THE SILVER LINING

THE SILVER LINING

11 PERSONALIZED SCRIPTURAL WAKE SERVICES
Dr. J. Massyngbaerde Ford

Fr. Gary Norman

TWENTY-THIRD PUBLICATIONS
Mystic, Connecticut

Scripture texts taken from the Jerusalem Bible, 1985 by Darton Longman
& Todd, Ltd. and Doubleday & Company, Inc.

Third Printing   *June, 1990*

Twenty-Third Publications
P.O. Box 180
Mystic, Ct 06355
(203) 536-2611

ISBN 0-89622-331-0
Library of Congress Catalog Card Number 87-50614

Cover design by Kathy Michalove
Book edited and designed by Mary Carol Kendzia

This book is dedicated to
LUCY MARGARET and WILLIAM HENRY McCULLOUGH,
both clothed in love
to whom the Son of Humanity will say,
"Come, you have my Father's blessing!
Inherit the kingdom prepared for you
from the creation of the world."
(Matthew 25:34)

Fr. Gary Norman

PREFACE

There is sacred healing power in sleep. Even contemporary scientists have no key to its mystery. It is not surprising that many peoples, including our Jewish forebears and the early Christians, spoke of the deceased as "those who had fallen asleep." For the ancients, it was of great importance that their loved ones be buried in the ground. They placed them and enfolded them in the arms of Mother Earth, who mysteriously died each winter and rose each spring. And for those who believed in the resurrection of the body the earth, as mother, conceived, carried, went into labor, and brought forth to life again those buried in her.

In this brief reflection I do not speak as a professional theologian but as a Christian who has faced death several times and who, in the meticulous providence of God, has learned something of the therapeutic potency of sleep.

I have suffered from severe and prolonged insomnia since I contracted milary tuberculosis in my twenties. Since the age of twenty-three I have never known a night of natural sleep.

But two years ago my cardiologist found medication to remedy this condition. It was then that I underwent a proleptic resurrection experience.

How wonderful—indeed, miraculous—has been the transformation. Not, of course, after one night's sleep, but throughout the past two years. New vistas of life have opened their welcoming arms to me.

If the sleep of life brings so much healing, how much more will the sleep of death transform the human person? It is not irrelevant that both Jews and Christ compare the difference between the natural and the resurrected body, respectively, to a seed "asleep in the earth" and fully grown corn transformed in its growth. Resurrection is no mere resuscitation of a corpse.

Thus with adequate, healing sleep we experience some of the following blessings:

— keener sense perception
— facility in personal relationships

- agility and vigor of the body
- increased mental comprehension and clarity
- more mobile sense of humor
- decrease in fear
- marked creative ability
- a deeper aesthetic appreciation
- a new dimension in prayer

In a similar way when one passes through the sleep of death, the body, which is the temple of the Holy Spirit, is quickened and the soul reaches new heights. The person becomes intimate with God and gains a deeper appreciation of all humanity.

May the services contained in this modest book be a source of comfort and hope for all whose loved ones have fallen asleep in the healing arms of God.

CONTENTS

THE SILVER LINING

For a Baby or Child

Introduction *(For the use of the presider and congregation before the service begins.)*

This service is arranged as follows: First, we are asked to reflect upon the humanity of Jesus. He experienced the range of human emotion, suffering, and joy. Thus the first reading is taken from the letter to the Hebrews, found in the New Testament. This letter presents a perfect balance between the human nature and the divine nature of Jesus. He approached his own death with fear and revulsion, but he went through the ordeal with faith and love. Then God raised him from the dead. We try to embrace this faith and love.

Our second reading, from the Gospel of Mark, shows that Jesus displayed anger and grief before God and before his human companions. We are invited to pour out our own grief before God, whose compassion and understanding surpasses all human imagination. The writers of the Old Testament psalms understood this very well, and the psalms display a wide range of human emotions, both negative and positive. Thus, we imitate the psalmists when we give expression to our grief, our loneliness, and our hope in God.

The third reading tells of King David, whose first-born son died in infancy. Though David was distraught with grief, he composed himself through his faith in God and returned to the activities of his daily life. God blessed him with another son who eventually became a prestigious king.

We try to comfort the parents by reminding them that they pleased God very much, and showed true Christian love and service when they attended to all the needs of this

1

child. Our fourth reading, from the Gospel of Matthew, portrays Jesus' coming on the day of judgment. Christ reveals all the deeds of loving kindness which the righteous have performed. With these words we can more clearly see what great love N. and N. *(name parents)* bestowed upon N. *(name the child)*.

Finally, we turn to intercession and thanksgiving, and remember the many children who have never known such love and comfort.

OPENING HYMN

WELCOME

PRESIDER   We are assembled today in grief, pain, and perhaps, anger. These were emotions fully experienced by Jesus, who is truly human and truly divine. Scripture describes his human emotions when he was faced with a painful and humiliating death. Jesus prayed to God. His prayer was answered, not because he was exempt from dying physically, but because, persevering in faith, he came through death to new life. Let us listen to these words of Scripture remembering that Jesus can fully emphasize with us.

FIRST READER   A reading from the letter to the Hebrews (5:7-9).

During his life on earth, he offered up prayer and entreaty, with loud cries and tears, to the one who had the power to save him from death, and, winning a hearing by his reverence, he learned obedience, Son though he was, through his sufferings; when he had been perfected, he became for all who obey him the source of eternal salvation and was acclaimed by God with the title of high priest of the order of Melchizedek.

This is the word of the Lord.

ALL   *Thanks be to God.*

PRESIDER   Therefore, in union with Jesus our brother, let us pour out our distress before God.

RESPONSORIAL *(Adapted from Psalm 102)*

PRESIDER   Yahweh, hear my prayer.
Let my cry for help reach you.
Do not turn away your face from me
when I am in trouble;
bend down and listen to me,
when I call, be quick to answer me!

ALL   *Jesus wept.*

PRESIDER   Like grass struck by blight, my heart is withering.
I forget to eat my meals...
I am like a desert-owl in the wastes,
a screech-owl among ruins,
I keep vigil and moan like a lone bird on a roof.

ALL   *Jesus wept.*

PRESIDER   My days are like a fading shadow,
I am withering up like grass.
But you, Yahweh, are enthroned for ever;
each generation in turn remembers you.
Rise up, take pity on Zion!
The time has come to have mercy on her,
the moment has come.

ALL   *Jesus wept.*

PRESIDER: This will be put on record for future generations,
and a people yet to be born shall praise God:
Yahweh has leaned down
from the heights of his sanctuary,
and looked down from heaven to earth,
to listen to the sighing of the captive,
and set free those condemned to death.

ALL   *Jesus wept.*

PRESIDER   Long ago you laid earth's foundations,
the heavens are the work of your hands.
They pass away but you remain:
they all wear out like a garment,
like outworn clothes you change them;
but you never alter, and your years never end.

ALL   *Jesus wept.*

PRESIDER   The children of those who serve you
will dwell secure,
and their descendants live on in your presence.

Psalm Prayer

PRESIDER   Let us pray:

God, our Father and Mother,
  you are patient and understanding with us
  in all our frailty.
Coax us to rely on your unchanging love,
  when we face the shortness of life
  and the swift removal of our joys.
We ask this through Jesus, our brother,

ALL   *Amen.*

PRESIDER   Friends, we have expressed our sorrow and pain.
Let us listen to the reaction of King David when his
first son became ill and died.

SECOND READER   A reading from the second book of Samuel (12:18-25).

On the seventh day the child died. David's retinue
were afraid to tell him that the child was dead. "Even
when the child was alive," they thought, "we reasoned
with him and he would not listen to us. How can
we tell him that the child is dead? He will do
something desperate." David, however, noticed that

his retinue were whispering among themselves, and realized that the child was dead. "Is the child dead?" he asked the officers. They replied, "He is dead."

David got off the ground, bathed and anointed himself and put on fresh clothes. Then he went into Yahweh's sanctuary and prostrated himself. On returning to his house, he asked to be served with food and ate it. His retinue said, "Why are you acting like this? When the child was alive, you fasted and wept; now that the child is dead, you get up and take food!" "When the child was alive," he replied, "I fasted and wept because I kept thinking, 'Who knows? Perhaps Yahweh will take pity on me and the child will live.' But now that he is dead, why should I fast? Can I bring him back again? I shall go to him but he cannot come back to me."

David consoled his wife Bathsheba. He went to her and slept with her. She conceived and gave birth to a son, whom she called Solomon. Yahweh loved him and made this known by means of the prophet Nathan, who named him Jedidiah, as Yahweh had instructed.

This is the word of the Lord.

ALL   *Thanks be to God.*

PRESIDER   Let us pray:

Holy Spirit, source of all understanding,
    fill our bereft and bewildered hearts
    with the warm breath of your consolation.
While N. (*name child*) was alive,
    we poured on her (him) all our love.
Let this be our quiet confidence:
    life is changed, not taken away.

ALL   *Amen.*

PRESIDER   God gave N. and N. (*name parents*) this little girl (boy), N. (*name child*). They bestowed on her (him) all their love. Let us reflect upon the words of Jesus who tells us that on Judgment Day every deed of loving kindness will be revealed, including all the deeds of loving kindness that N. and N. did for N.

THIRD READER   A reading from the Gospel of Matthew (25:31-37; 40).

When the Son of man comes in his glory, escorted by all the angels, then he will take his seat on his throne of glory. All nations will be assembled before him and he will separate people from one another as the shepherd separates sheep from goats. He will place the sheep on his right hand and the goats on his left. Then the king will say to those on his right hand, "Come, you whom my Father has blessed, take as your heritage the kingdom prepared for you since the foundation of the world. For I was hungry and you gave me food, I was thirsty and you gave me drink, I was a stranger and you made me welcome, lacking clothes and you clothed me, sick and you visited me, in prison and you came to see me.

In truth I tell you, in so far as you did this to one of the least of these brothers (and sisters) of mine, you did it to me."

This is the word of the Lord.

ALL   *Thanks be to God.*

PRAYER

FIRST READER   Let us bless God, because when N. was hungry,

SECOND READER   N. and N. gave N. food.

FIRST READER   When she (he) was thirsty,

SECOND READER   They gave her (him) to drink.

FIRST READER   When she (he) was naked,

Second Reader   They clothed her (him) and they gave her (him) a home full of love.

First Reader   In this they have shown themselves to be true disciples of Jesus,

Second Reader   For which we bless God.

Prayer of Intercession and Thanksgiving

Presider   Let us thank God for the gift of this child and offer our petitions to God.

That, as N. was reborn in the waters of baptism, she (he) may enjoy eternal happiness in heaven,

All   *Merciful Lord, hear us.*

Presider   For the consolation of this family and their friends,

All   *Merciful Lord, hear us.*

Presider   That we may be patient with ourselves when we are visited with anguish or despair,

All   *Merciful Lord, hear us.*

Presider   In thanksgiving for all the joy, happiness and tenderness which N. gave her (his) family in her (his) short life,

All   *Merciful Lord, hear us.*

Presider   That we may realize that N.'s life is changed, not taken away,

All   *Merciful Lord, hear us.*

(A time here is given for personal reflection, intercession, or thanksgiving, either silent or vocal. After a suitable time the presider can close the prayers.)

COLLECT

PRESIDER   Let us pray for all the children who have lived
and died in unloving circumstances.

FIRST READER   For those who have died of starvation,

SECOND READER   Lord, nourish them at your heavenly banquet.

FIRST READER   For those who have died through lack of water,

SECOND READER   Lord, give them the living water.

FIRST READER   For those who have died without homes,

SECOND READER   Lord, welcome them to your many mansions.

FIRST READER   For those who died without human love,

SECOND READER   Lord, enfold them in your arms.

FIRST READER   For those who died through the brutality
of war or crime,

SECOND READER   Lord, grant them your everlasting peace.

PRESIDER   Jesus, our Lord and our brother,
judge of the living and the dead,
through your death you won
eternal life for us.
Grant to us all unflinching faith.
May we be confident that we shall meet N. once
more on the day of resurrection.
Then every tear will be replaced with joy and peace.

ALL   *Amen.*

DISMISSAL AND BLESSING

PRESIDER   Go in peace and remember
the kingdom of heaven is like a child.

ALL   *Thanks be to God.*

PRESIDER   May God lift up his countenance and give us peace.
            May God help us to comfort one another,
                may God help us to remember N.
                not with sorrow but with joy.

ALL   *Amen.*

CLOSING HYMN

For The Elderly

INTRODUCTION   *(For the use of the presider and congregation before the service begins.)*

The passing of an elderly person into eternal life is not necessarily a time for mourning as much as a time of happiness and peace. The readings have been chosen with this in mind.

The opening psalm celebrates God's companionship and love from birth to the "coming of age."

The second reading is a well-known passage from the book of Ecclesiasticus. It commemorates men and women who have risen as leaders in their communities through their various skills, yet it also remembers those who were precious in God's eyes but little known to the human community.

The third reading from the Gospel of John speaks clearly about the raising of the dead by Jesus.

The service ends with the traditional evening hymn from Scripture, the *Nunc Dimittis* (Now Lettest Thou). These are the words of Simeon, who asked God to show him the Messiah before he died. When Jesus was presented as a baby in the temple at Jerusalem, Simeon felt that the desire of his heart was fulfilled and that now he could be called to God.

OPENING HYMN

WELCOME

PRESIDER   N. *(name deceased)* was called by God in ripeness of years. In the words of Isaiah:

"You have folded up my life, like a weaver
who severs the last thread."
And in the book of Job we read:
"You shall approach the grave in full vigor,
as a shock of grain comes in at its season."

Let us give thanks for the divine love and support
which N. received in her (his) lifetime.

RESPONSORIAL   (*Adapted from Psalm 71*)

PRESIDER In you, Yahweh, I take refuge...
Be a sheltering rock for me,
always accessible;
you have determined to save me,
for you are my rock, my fortress.

ALL *Comfort me over and over.*

PRESIDER For you are my hope, Lord,
my trust, Yahweh, since childhood.
On you I have relied since my birth,
since my mother's womb you have been my portion,
the constant theme of my praise.

ALL *Comfort me over and over.*

PRESIDER Do not reject me in my old age,
nor desert me when my strength is failing...
My lips shall proclaim your saving justice,
your saving power all day long.

ALL *Comfort me over and over.*

PRESIDER God, you have taught me from childhood,
and I am still praising your marvels.
Now that I am old and grey-haired,
God, do not desert me,
till I have proclaimed your strength
to generations still to come,
your power and justice to the skies.

ALL *Comfort me over and over.*

PSALM PRAYER

PRESIDER   O God, our Creator and Preserver,
we give you thanks for the loving care
which you continually bestowed upon N.
Comfort those who grieve.
Let them rest in the assurance
that your love for N. is not totally fulfilled,
and she (he) is cradled in pure joy,
through Jesus Christ, our Lord,

ALL   *Amen.*

PRESIDER   Let us listen to a reading from the Old Testament
which praises good men and women, both professional persons and those who work in other occupa-
tions. Let us recall that N. devoted herself (himself)
to (*name deceased's occupation*).

*(A symbol of N.'s occupation or things in which she (he)
took delight may be placed on the coffin or "altar.")*

FIRST READER   A reading from the book of Ecclesiasticus (44:1-15).

Next let us praise illustrious people,
   our ancestors in their successive generations.
The Lord has created an abundance of glory,
   and displayed his greatness from earliest times.
Some wielded authority as kings,
   and were renowned for their strength;
others were intelligent advisers
   and uttered prophetic sayings.
Others directed people by their advice,
   by their understanding of the popular mind,
   and by the wise words of their teaching;
others composed musical melodies
   and set down ballads;
others were rich and powerful,
   living peaceably in their homes.

All these were honored by their contemporaries
    and were the glory of their day.
Some of them left a name behind them,
    so that their praises are still sung.
While others have left no memory
    and disappeared as though they had never existed.
They are now as though they had never been,
    and so too, their children after them.

And here is a list of illustrious people
    whose good works have not been forgotten.
In their descendants they find
    a rich inheritance, their posterity.
Their descendants stand by the commandments
    and, thanks to them,
    so do their children's children.
Their offspring will last forever,
    their glory will not fade.
Their bodies have been buried in peace,
    and their name lives on for all generations.
The peoples will proclaim their wisdom,
    the assembly will celebrate their praises.

This is the word of the Lord.

ALL   *Thanks be to God.*

PSALM PRAYER

PRESIDER   God, our Creator and Sanctifer,
    we bless you for all that makes life
    handsome and kind.
May the contribution to life
    which N. made through your Spirit,
    be for us comfort, strength, and inspiration,
    through Jesus Christ, our Lord,

ALL   *Amen.*

PRESIDER   Let us listen to the good news of salvation brought by our Savior, Jesus Christ.

SECOND READER   A reading from the Gospel of John (5:19-21; 24-30).

To this Jesus replied:
In all truth I tell you,
by himself the Son can do nothing;
he can do only what he sees the Father doing;
and whatever the Father does the Son does too.
For the Father loves the Son
and shows him everything he himself does,
and he will show him even greater things than these,
works that will astonish you.
Thus, as the Father raises the dead and gives them
     life,
so the Son gives life to anyone he chooses...

In all truth I tell you,
whoever listens to my words,
and believes in the one who sent me,
has eternal life;
without being brought to judgment
such a person has passed from death to life.
In all truth I tell you,
the hour is coming—indeed it is already here—
when the dead will hear the voice of the Son of God,
and all who hear it will live.
For as the Father has life in himself,
so he has granted the Son also to have life in himself;
and, because he is the Son of man,
has granted him power to give judgment.
Do not be surprised at this,
for the hour is coming
when the dead will leave their graves
at the sound of his voice:
those who did good
will come forth to life;
and those who did evil will come forth to judgment.

This is the word of the Lord.

ALL   *Thanks be to God.*

PRESIDER   God of comfort and support,
    we pray for those friends of N.
    who have come of age.
When their hour comes,
    may they go forth with peace of soul,
    with comfort of body
    and clarity and serenity of mind.
May they lift smiling eyes of expectation towards Jesus,
    who was the first to rise from the dead.

ALL   *Amen.*

PRAYER OF INTERCESSION AND THANKSGIVING

PRESIDER   We have heard God's pleasure in good men and women. Let us offer our thanksgiving and petitions to God, and be mindful of N.'s joy and patience in work and in recreation.

For N.'s delight in her (his) devotion to. . .(name occupation), may her (his) example be followed by many, let us pray to God,

ALL   *Creator, hear our prayer*

PRESIDER   For N.'s enjoyment of recreation, especially *(name deceased's hobbies and activities)*, let us thank our God,

ALL   *Creator, hear our prayer.*

PRESIDER   For N.'s love and concern for family and friends *(name family and special friends)*, let us give thanks to our God,

ALL   *Creator, hear our prayer.*

PRESIDER   For the good health and the material, psychological, and spiritual blessings of N., let us thank our God,

(Or: For N'.s patience and endurance in illness and suf-
fering, let us thank our God,)

ALL   *Creator, hear our prayer.*

PRESIDER   For all those who are bereaved and desolate by the
death of N., that God will comfort and support
them, let us pray to our God,

ALL   *Creator, hear our prayer.*

PRESIDER   For the repose of N.'s soul, let us pray to our God.

ALL   *Creator, hear our prayer.*

PRESIDER   Friends, we invite you to offer petitions and thanks
in your own words.

(A time is offered for personal spontaneous prayer.)

PRESIDER   Let us pray:

O God, our Creator and our Savior,
    we bless you for the many gifts and talents,
    the hopes, fears, successes, and failures,
    which N. shared with us.
May we cherish them as a memorial,
    may we build on the foundation
    which she (he) laid down,
    through Jesus Christ, our brother,

ALL   *Amen.*

COLLECT

PRESIDER   Let us pray:

God of hope and comfort,
    you gave your only Son for our redemption.
Through his cross and resurrection
    support us through the valley
    of the shadow of death.

Lead us to commune with you face to face,
    as friend to friend;
Through Jesus Christ, our Lord and brother,

ALL   *Amen.*

PRESIDER   Let us express our farewell to N. in the words of Simeon, the priest, when he saw the infant Jesus in the temple at Jerusalem;

Now, Master, you are letting your servant go in
    peace
as you promised;
for my eyes have seen the salvation
which you have made ready in the sight of the
    nations;
a light of revelation for the gentiles
and glory for your people Israel.

DISMISSAL AND BLESSING

PRESIDER   Go in peace,
    to cherish the memory of N.,

ALL   *Thanks be to God.*

PRESIDER   The grace of our Lord Jesus Christ,
    and the love of God,
    and the fellowship of the Holy Spirit
    be with you all,

ALL   *Amen.*

CLOSING HYMN

FOR YOUNG MEN AND WOMEN

INTRODUCTION   *(For the use of the presider and congregation while waiting for the service to begin.)*

This wake is designed for more than one young man or woman who have died together, e.g., in a car accident. However, it may be adapted for one young person.

The first reading is thought to be the oldest lamentation in Hebrew Scriptures. It describes David's heartfelt grief when he lost his closest friend, Jonathan, and Saul, his king. Both had died in the same battle.

The second reading is taken from one of the later books of the Old Testament. It describes how, during a devastating persecution of the Jews, a mother lost seven sons in one day. She was able to cope with the situation because of her staunch belief in the resurrection of the dead.

The responsorial is taken from St. Paul's letter to the Corinthians in which he speaks at length about the resurrection of Jesus and our own future resurrection. He is addressing the Corinthians, who seem to have believed in the immortality of the soul but not the resurrection of the whole person. He explains that the resurrection of the body is not just the resuscitation of a corpse but a transformed body, transformed just as a seed is changed into fully grown wheat.

The last reading is taken from the Gospel of John. In it we hear how Lazarus, who was a close friend of Jesus, fell ill and died. Jesus went to Lazarus' family, who were also close friends, and comforted them. He then raised Lazarus from the dead. This was a brave action on the part of Jesus, because eventually, it led directly to his own death on the cross.

The response to this reading is taken from the epistle to the Hebrews, which speaks about the joy and festivity of human beings when they go to heaven.

Opening Hymn

Welcome

Presider   Friends, death has made a sudden and violent intrusion into our lives. It has snatched life from those who enjoyed youth and strength, and who were buoyed up with the hope, excitement, and challenge of life. Let us express our anguish in the words of David who, in one day, lost both his king, Saul, and his closest friend, Jonathan.

Responsorial Psalm   *(Adapted from 2 Samuel 1:19-27. The names of the deceased may be substituted for "Saul and Jonathan.)*

Presider   Does the splendor of Israel
lie dead on your heights?
How did the heroes fall?

All   *Saul and Jonathan, beloved and cherished,*
Separated neither in life nor in death.

Presider   Do not speak of it in Gath,
nor broadcast it in the streets of Ashkelon,
for fear the daughters of the Philistines rejoice,
for fear the daughters of the uncircumcised gloat.

All   *Saul and Jonathan, beloved and cherished,*
Separated neither in life nor in death.

Presider   You mountains of Gilboa,
no dew, no rain fall on you,
O treacherous fields
where the heroes' shield lies dishonored!

All   *Saul and Jonathan, beloved and cherished,*
Separated neither in life nor in death.

Presider   Saul and Jonathan, beloved and handsome,
were divided neither in life, nor in death.

> Swifter than eagles were they,
> stronger than lions.

ALL *Saul and Jonathan, beloved and cherished,*
Separated neither in life nor in death.

PSALM PRAYER

PRESIDER God, our Father and our Mother,
your only Son was stricken with cruel death
in the vigor of his youth.
Give us strength to face this bereavement;
be patient with our grief and anger.
In this crucible of suffering
refine within us the fruits of the Spirit.

ALL *Amen.*

PRESIDER My friends, God calls us to heroic courage and unrivaled hope. Let us reflect upon the words of Scripture concerning the noble mother who lost seven sons in one day. Her faith rises from a deep conviction of God as creator, and one who raises the dead.

FIRST READER A reading from the second book of Maccabees (7:20-23).

But the mother was especially admirable and worthy of honorable rememberance, for she watched the death of seven sons in the course of a single day, and bravely endured it because of her hopes in the Lord. Indeed she encouraged each of them in their ancestral tongue; filled with noble conviction, she reinforced her womanly argument with manly courage, saying to them, "I do not know how you appeared in my womb; it was not I who endowed you with breath and life, I had not the shaping of your every part. And hence, the Creator of the world, who made everyone and ordained the origin of all things, will in his mercy give you back breath and life, since for the sake of his laws you have no concern for yourselves."

This is the word of the Lord.

All   *Thanks be to God.*

Presider   Let us pray:

O God, you created and elected us,
    each with his or her destiny
    in life and in death.
Be present among us and breathe into us
    the strength of your spirit.
May the mysteries which we cannot understand
    now be kept in our hearts in faith
    until that day when all will be understood
    in the presence of the divine,
    through Jesus Christ, our Lord,

All   *Amen.*

Presider   We live in sure and certain hope of the resurrection of the dead because Jesus, our Lord and brother, truly died and truly rose from the dead. Let us profess this faith and be not as those who have no hope.

Prayer *(Adapted from 1 Corinthians 15)*

First Reader   If there is no resurrection of the dead,

Second Reader   Christ himself has not been raised.

First Reader   And if Christ has not been raised,

Second Reader   Our preaching is void of content and your faith is empty, too...and those who have fallen asleep in Christ are the deadest of the dead.

First Reader   If our hopes in Christ are limited to this life only,

Second Reader   We are the most pitiable of human beings.

FIRST READER   But as it is, Christ is now raised from the dead,

SECOND READER   The first fruits of those who have fallen asleep.

FIRST READER   Just as in Adam all die,

SECOND READER   So in Christ all will come to life again.

PRESIDER   Let us hear with joy a reading from the gospel according to John. Jesus raised his beloved friend Lazarus from the dead. N. and N. *(name deceased)* are already given their resurrected bodies. They have entered a life of joy and discovery which no human mind can conceive. Let us pray for the faith to believe this.

SECOND READER   A reading from the Gospel of John (11:17-27).

On arriving, Jesus found that Lazarus had been in the tomb for four days already. Bethany was only about two miles from Jerusalem, and many Jews had come to Martha and Mary to comfort them about their brother. When Martha heard that Jesus was coming she went to meet him. Mary remained sitting in the house. Martha said to Jesus, "Lord, if you had been here, my brother would not have died, but even now I know that God will grant whatever you ask of him." Jesus said to her, "Your brother will rise again." Martha said, "I know he will rise again at the resurrection on the last day." Jesus said;

"I am the resurrection.
Anyone who believes in me, even though
that person dies, will live,
and whoever lives and believes in me
will never die.
Do you believe this?"

"Yes, Lord," she said, "I believe that you are the Christ, the Son of God, the one who was to come into this world."

This is the word of the Lord.

Fr. Gary Norman

ALL   *Thanks be to God.*

PRESIDER   Let us pray:

Jesus, our Savior,
   you raised the son of the widow of Naim,
   the daughter of Jairus,
   and Lazarus, your friend.
Visit us with your spirit
   so that we may truly believe that N. and N.
   have attained eternal life
   where there is no pain or sorrow
   but only joy and discovery.

ALL   *Amen.*

PRAYER

FIRST READER   They dwell in the city of the living God

SECOND READER   Among myriads of angels in festal gathering;

FIRST READER   The assembly of the first-born enrolled in heaven,

SECOND READER   With God who is judge of all.

FIRST READER   With the spirits of just men and women made perfect,

SECOND READER   With Jesus, the mediator of a new covenant,

FIRST READER   They have been sprinkled with the blood of Jesus,

SECOND READER   Which speaks more eloquently than that of Abel.

PRESIDER   May Jesus' blood cleanse us from all sin
   and bring us all to everlasting life.

ALL   *Amen.*

PRAYER OF INTERCESSION AND THANKSGIVING

PRESIDER   Let us offer our petitions and thanksgiving to God.

For the repose of the souls of N. and N., that they may be joined to the communion of saints,

ALL   *Creator, hear our prayer.*

PRESIDER   In thanksgiving for the enthusiasm, generosity, and service of these young people, let us pray to the Lord,

ALL   *Creator, hear our prayer.*

PRESIDER   That memory of the moments of joy with these young people may be as treasured and poignant as their loss, let us pray to the Lord,

ALL   *Creator, hear our prayer.*

PRESIDER   For their families, their friends, and their companions at work that healing and adjustment to their loss will gradually ease their fierce grief, let us pray to the Lord,

ALL   *Creator, hear our prayer.*

PRESIDER   For the faith and realization that N. and N. have passed, not to death, but to a fuller and more enriching life, let us pray to the Lord,

ALL   *Creator, hear our prayer.*

(Here the congregation is invited to add their prayers for the bereaved, and also in thanksgiving for the special gifts of the deceased persons, e.g., in the arts, in service, in education, or in athletics. These intercessions can be written in advance with the help of the family.)

COLLECT *(Commemoration of forgotten youths.)*

PRESIDER   In our grief let us not forget those who died without the blessings which our friends enjoyed.

FIRST READER   For the young men and women whose lives have been destroyed by war and violence,

SECOND READER   Loving God, grant them the prosperity of peace.

FIRST READER   For the young who died without experiencing good health and vigor,

SECOND READER   Loving God, grant them joy in the vigor of their transformed bodies.

FIRST READER   For the young who died without education and learning,

SECOND READER   Loving God, grant them the adventure of wisdom and understanding.

FIRST READER   For the young who died without friends,

SECOND READER   Loving God, grant them the felicity of the communion of saints,

ALL   *Amen.*

PRESIDER   God, our Creator and Redeemer,
grant us grace, that even in grief
we may give thanks for the treasures of these
young lives.
May we not fail them.
May we seek to promote all the good things of life
which they cherished.

ALL   *Amen.*

DISMISSAL AND BLESSING

PRESIDER   Go in peace
and be ever youthful
in your own lives.

ALL   *Amen.*

PRESIDER   The grace of the Lord Jesus Christ,
           and the love of God,
           and the fellowship of the Holy Spirit
           be with you all.

ALL   *Amen.*

CLOSING HYMN

For a Friend

INTRODUCTION *(For the use of the presider and the congregation while waiting for the service to begin)*

Friendship is given special emphasis in both the Old and New Testaments. This service first recalls that Jesus himself valued and needed human friendship, and was devastated when a friend betrayed him. The psalm commemorates the friendship of God, especially towards those in distress.

Our first reading comes from the book of Ecclesiasticus. It speaks about prudence in selecting friends and the qualities which are truly precious in friendship. The responsorial continues the same theme but particularly emphasizes lasting friendship, and friendship in times of adversity.

The second reading is from the Gospel of John. It tells how Jesus promised that he would prepare a place in heaven for his friends, for he does not call us servants or slaves but friends.

OPENING HYMN

WELCOME

PRESIDER Brothers and sisters, in his gospel John writes that when Lazarus' sisters, Martha and Mary, told Jesus of the illness of their brother they said: "Lord, the one you love is sick."

The evangelist adds: "Jesus loved Martha and her sister and Lazarus very much." John reports that when Jesus came to his friend's tomb he wept.

Realizing that Jesus can empathize with our loss because he also had close friends, let us express our grief in the words of Scripture.

RESPONSORIAL PSALM *(Adapted from Psalm 40)*

PRESIDER I waited, I waited for Yahweh,
then he stooped to me
and heard my cry for help.

ALL *God stooped towards me and heard my cry.*

PRESIDER He pulled me up from the seething chasm,
from the mud of the mire.
He set my feet on rock,
and made my footsteps firm.

ALL *God stooped towards me and heard my cry.*

PRESIDER How blessed are those
who put their trust in Yahweh,
How much you have done,
Yahweh, my God—
your wonders, your plans for us—
you have no equal.
I will proclaim and speak of them;
they are beyond number.

ALL *God stooped towards me and heard my cry.*

PRESIDER You, Yahweh, have not withheld
your tenderness from me;
your faithful and steadfast love
will always guard me.

ALL *God stooped towards me and heard my cry.*

PRESIDER Poor and needy as I am,
the Lord has me in mind.
You, my helper, my Savior
my God, do not delay.

ALL *God stooped towards me and heard my cry.*

PSALM PRAYER

PRESIDER   O, God, our friend,
            make us glad for the faithful witness
            of our friend N. (*name deceased*).
            Let us treasure the fruits of the Spirit
            which we saw dwelling in him (her)
            and receive them as an inheritance
            to be shared and enjoyed
            by our families and communities.

ALL   *Amen.*

PRESIDER   We realize that Jesus can empathize with our loss because he, too, had close friends, both men and women. Let us listen to the words of Scripture about true friendship.

FIRST READER   A reading from the book of Ecclesiasticus (6:5-17). *(The feminine pronoun may be substituted for the masculine when the deceased is a woman.)*

A kindly turn of speech attracts new friends,
    a courteous tongue invites many a friendly
    response.
Let your acquaintances be many, but for advisers
    choose one out of a thousand.
If you want to make a friend, take him on trial,
    and do not be in a hurry to trust him;
for one kind of friend is so only when it suits him
    but will not stand by you in your day of trouble.

Keep well clear of your enemies,
    and be wary of your friends.
A loyal friend is a powerful defense:
    whoever finds one has indeed found a treasure.
A loyal friend is something beyond price,
    there is no measuring his worth.
A loyal friend is the elixir of life,
    and those who fear the Lord will find one.

Whoever fears the Lord makes true friends,
for as a person is, so is his friend, too.

This is the word of the Lord.

ALL   *Thanks be to God.*

PRESIDER   God, our true friend,
we give you sincere thanks
for our friendship with N.
In honor of him (her)
grant that our conversation
may always be gracious,
our conduct honorable,
and our friendships sincere.

ALL   *Amen.*

PRAYER

FIRST READER   Discard not an old friend,
for the new one cannot equal him (her).

SECOND READER   A new friend is like a new wine
which you drink with pleasure
only when it has aged.

FIRST READER   A friend is always a friend;

SECOND READER   A brother is born for the time of stress.

FIRST READER   A brother is a better defense than a strong city, and
a friend is like the bars of a castle.

SECOND READER   Some friends bring ruin on us,
but a true friend is more loyal than a brother.

FIRST READER   Before you die be good to your friend,
and give him (her) a share in what you possess.

PRESIDER   Let us pray:

O God, you were the intimate friend of Moses,
the one to whom he complained,

the one to whom he gave thanks.
We thank you for the gift of this friend
    who has supported us in many times of stress
    and celebrated with us in many times of joy:
    a friend tested like gold in a furnace.
May he (she) rest in peace
    and may we have peace even in sorrow,
    through Jesus Christ, our friend and brother,

ALL   *Amen.*

PRESIDER   Let us hear how Jesus speaks of a unique friendship between God and human beings.

SECOND READER   A reading from the Gospel of John (15:12-17).

This is my commandment:
Love one another,
as I have loved you.
No one can have greater love
than to lay down his (her) life for his (her) friends.
You are my friends,
if you do what I command you.
I shall no longer call you servants,
because a servant does not know
the master's business;
I call you friends,
because I have made known to you
everything I have learned from my Father.
You did not choose me,
no, I chose you;
and I commissioned you
to go out and to bear fruit,
fruit that will last;
so that the Father will give you
anything you ask him in my name.
My command to you
is to love one another.

This is the word of the Lord.

ALL   *Thanks be to God.*

PRESIDER   Let us respond to this reading by reflecting on the nature of Christian love as described by Paul the Apostle.

FIRST READER   If I speak with human tongues and angelic as well, but do not have love,

SECOND READER   I am a noisy gong, a clanging cymbal.

FIRST READER   Love is patient: love is kind. Love is not jealous, it does not put on airs, it is not snobbish.

SECOND READER   Love is never rude, it is not self-seeking, it is not prone to anger; neither does it brood over injuries.

FIRST READER   Love does not rejoice in what is wrong but rejoices with the truth.

SECOND READER   There is no limit to love's forbearance, to its trust, its hope, its power to endure.

FIRST READER   There are in the end three things which last: faith, hope and love,

SECOND READER   And the greatest of these is love.

PRAYER OF INTERCESSION AND THANKSGIVING

PRESIDER   Let us thank God for the graces and excellent qualities of N. and ask for the grace to imitate them.

For the repose of the soul of N. that he (she) may rejoice in the eternal friendship of God, let us pray to the Lord,

ALL   *Gracious friend, hear our prayer.*

PRESIDER   That when we celebrate the eucharist we may experience the fellowship of the Church triumphant which now embraces our friend, let us pray to the Lord,

ALL   *Gracious friend, hear our prayer.*

PRESIDER In thanksgiving for the gifts and fruits of the Holy Spirit which were revealed in N., let us pray to the Lord,

ALL   *Gracious friend, hear our prayer.*

PRESIDER That the tragedy of the loss of N. may knit our families and our friendship together, let us pray to the Lord,

ALL   *Gracious friend, hear our prayer.*

PRESIDER That when we touch or see possessions which belonged to N. we may remember the privilege of his (her) friendship, let us pray to the Lord,

ALL   *Gracious friend, hear our prayer.*

(Here the presider invites spontaneous prayer, and after a suitable pause prays:)

PRESIDER O God, your Son laid down his life for his friends,
teach us wherein true friendship lies,
so that our deceased friend's name
may be hallowed.

ALL   *Amen.*

COLLECT *(Prayer for the forgotten)*

PRESIDER Let us pray:

FIRST READER For those to whom friendship brought pain:
for those who died in the absence of friends;

SECOND READER May God grant them eternal friendship.

FIRST READER For friends who have been divided by war and violence, especially if they found themselves on opposing sides;

SECOND READER   May God's healing power grant them reconciliation.

FIRST READER   For those whose nuptial friendship has been disrupted,

SECOND READER   May God bring them together in love and peace.

PRESIDER   Let us join in the prayer which Jesus taught us:

ALL   *Our father... (continue prayer)*

DISMISSAL AND BLESSING

PRESIDER   Go in peace to befriend man, woman, child
and all creatures great and small.

ALL   *Thanks be to God.*

PRESIDER   May God grant us wisdom,
the pure effluence of his glory,
that God, who is one,
may renew everything;
and, passing into holy souls from age to age,
make them friends of God and prophets.

(Or: May your friends be as the sun
rising in its might!)

(Or: The friendship of the Lord
is with those who fear him,
and his covenant, for their instruction.)

ALL   *Amen.*

CLOSING HYMN

FOR A MOTHER

INTRODUCTION   *(For the presider and congregation as they wait for the service to begin.)*

Scripture uses the image of trees and vines to speak of motherhood, because a mother shelters and nourishes her family. Scripture also personifies Wisdom as a woman. In the Old Testament the Spirit of God is spoken of in the feminine gender.

The opening prayer comes from Jesus' farewell discourses to his disciples. Here he uses the image of the vine to explain the relationship between him and his disciples who were both men and women. A mother has a similar relationship to her family.

The first reading is taken from Isaiah. It compares the love of God to the love of a woman for her child.

The second reading speaks about the pre-existence of Wisdom, personified as a woman, who cooperates with with God in creating the cosmos.

The third reading is from the Gospel of John, again from the farewell discourses. Jesus went to prepare a place in heaven for his disciples. The woman for whom we mourn today goes to prepare a place for her loved ones.

The service ends with a paraphrase of Mary's song of thanksgiving after her conception of Jesus, when Elizabeth greeted her as the "mother of her Lord."

OPENING HYMN

WELCOME

PRESIDER   Friends, we come together to mourn the death of a mother. A mother, in a special way, reflects the

35

love of God. Jesus himself revealed his maternal love for his people when he said:

> How often have I wanted to gather your children together as a mother bird collects her young under her wings... (Luke 13:34).

Jesus also used a maternal image when he proclaimed that he was the vine and we the branches. The vine is the nourishment and support of the branches. Let us reflect on this Scripture text as we intermingle it with the words of the prophet Ezekiel, who used this image in describing Israel.

RESPONSORIAL *(Adapted from John:15; and Ezekiel 19:10-11)*

PRESIDER   I am the true vine,
and my Father is the vinedresser.
Every branch in me that bears no fruit
he cuts away,
and every branch that does bear fruit he prunes
to make it bear even more.

ALL   *Your mother was like a vine*
Planted beside the water.

PRESIDER   You are clean already,
by means of the word that I have spoken to you.
Remain in me, as I in you,
As a branch cannot bear fruit all by itself,
unless it remains part of the vine,
neither can you unless you remain in me.

ALL   *Your mother was like a vine*
Planted beside the water.

PRESIDER   I am the vine,
you are the branches.
Whoever remains in me, and I in them
bears fruit in plenty;
for cut off from me you can do nothing.

ALL   *Your mother was like a vine*
Planted beside the water.

PRESIDER   Remain in my love.
If you keep my commandments
you will remain in my love,
just as I have kept my Father's commandments
and remain in his love.

ALL   *Your mother was like a vine*
Planted beside the water.

PRESIDER   I have told you this
so that my own joy will be in you
and your joy may be complete.
My Father has been glorified
in your bearing much fruit
and becoming my disciples.

ALL   *Your mother was like a vine*
Planted beside the water.

PRESIDER   Fruitful and branchy was she
because of abundant water.
One strong branch she put out
as a royal scepter.
Stately was her height
amid the dense foliage;
Notably tall was she
with her many clusters.

ALL   *Your mother was like a vine*
Planted beside the water.

PSALM PRAYER

PRESIDER   O God, our Father and our Mother,
make us truly grateful for,
and give us glad memories
of our deceased mother, N. *(name deceased)*.
We thank you for her love,
her support, her understanding, and

her example of Christian motherhood.
May her spirit ever abide with us.

ALL   *Amen.*

PRESIDER   Friends, in our sorrow let us meditate upon God's
unfailing maternal love expressed in the words of
the prophet Isaiah.

FIRST READER   A reading from the book of Isaiah (49:15-16; 66:13;
and 54:7-8, 10).

Can a woman forget her baby at the breast,
feel no pity for the child she has borne?
Even if these were to forget,
I shall not forget you.
Look, I have engraved you on the palms of my
   hands.

As a mother comforts a child,
so I shall comfort you;
you will be comforted in Jerusalem.
I did forsake you for a brief moment,
but in great compassion I shall take you back.
In a flood of anger, for a moment
I hid my face from you,
But with everlasting love I have taken pity on you,
says Yahweh, your redeemer.

For the mountains may go away
and the hills may totter,
but my faithful love will never leave you,
my covenant of peace will never totter,
says Yahweh who takes pity on you.

This is the word of the Lord.

ALL   *Thanks be to God.*

PRESIDER   Spirit of God, you are the source
   of all comfort. You are the parent of orphans.
Comfort us in our bereavement,

help us to give and receive
consolation from each other.
Grant that this mournful occasion
may be one of growth
and increased responsibility,
through Jesus Christ, our brother,

All   *Amen.*

Presider   Friends, in the Old Testament both Wisdom and the
Holy Spirit are personified as women. Let us reflect
upon the intellectual and spiritual gifts possessed by
N.

Second Reader   A reading from the book of Proverbs (8:22-31).

Yahweh created me, first-fruits of his fashioning,
    before the oldest of his works.
From everlasting, I was firmly set,
    from the beginning, before the earth
        came into being.
The deep was not, when I was born,
    nor were the springs with their abounding waters.
Before the mountains were settled,
    before the hills, I came to birth;
before he had made the earth, the countryside,
    and the first elements of the world.
When he fixed the heavens firm, I was there,
    when he drew a circle on the surface of the deep,
when he thickened the clouds above,
    when the sources of the deep began to swell,
when he assigned the sea its boundaries,
    —and the waters will not encroach on the shore—
    when he traced the foundations of the earth,
I was beside the master craftsman,
    delighting him day after day,
    ever at play in his presence,
at play everywhere on his earth,
    delighting to be with the children of men
    and women.

ALL   *Thanks be to God.*

PRESIDER   God of wisdom,
   you endow with your Spirit
   both man and woman.
  Enable us to follow in the footsteps of N.
   to whom you gave wisdom and understanding.

ALL   *Amen.*

THIRD READER   A reading from the Gospel of John (14:1-4).

  Do not let your hearts be troubled.
  You trust in God, trust also in me.
  In my Father's house there are many places to live in;
  otherwise I would have told you.
  I am going now to prepare a place for you,
  and after I have gone and prepared you a place,
  I shall return to take you to myself,
  so that you may be with me
  where I am.
  You know the way to the place where I am going.

  This is the word of the Lord.

ALL   *Thanks be to God.*

PRESIDER   Jesus, our brother,
   give us faith to believe
   that N. has been welcomed into her heavenly
    home.
  She waits for us to join her
   when our gracious God calls.

ALL   *Amen.*

PRAYER OF INTERCESSION AND THANKSGIVING

PRESIDER   Let us present our intercessions to God who is alert
  to hear the cry of the bereaved:

For the repose of the soul of N., may she rest in peace, and find the fulfillment of that new life which was given to her in baptism.

ALL   *God, our Creator, hear us.*

PRESIDER   In thanksgiving for the special gifts of N. *(here some may be specified)*, for her professional achievement which she combined with her love for her family, may she ever be an inspiration for us,

ALL   *God, our Creator, hear us.*

PRESIDER   For her enjoyment of leisure *(here some activities may be specified)*, may we follow her role model in work and recreation,

ALL   *God, our Creator, hear us.*

PRESIDER   For her husband, N., and her children, N. and N., may the Holy Spirit console them

ALL   *God, our Creator, hear us.*

PRESIDER   For us that we may believe that N. continues to live and takes an interest and delight in our lives,

ALL   *God, our Creator, hear us.*

(Here the presider invites spontaneous prayer, and after a suitable pause prays:)

PRESIDER   God of love,
        may that love which we received from N.
        be nurtured within us,
    so that we ourselves may extend compassion
        towards' a love-starved world,
        through Jesus Christ, our brother.

ALL   *Amen.*

COLLECT *(Prayer for the forgotten)*

PRESIDER   Let us pray for marriage partners who have not been blessed as we have.

FIRST READER   For the childless,

SECOND READER   May God bless them with fertility.

FIRST READER   For parents separated from their children,

SECOND READER   May God grant the happiness of a re-united family.

FIRST READER   For parents bereaved by war and violence,

SECOND READER   May they be granted the peace which passes all understanding.

PRESIDER   Let us conclude with a modern form of the song of Mary, the mother of Jesus.

And, I, in the dignity of Christian womanhood, say:
My soul does magnify our God
and my spirit rejoices in God my savior,
for, in my human fraility, the Spirit, our Mother,
has chosen me.
For, behold, from now on all generations will bless
her gift within me.
For she who is all powerful has empowered me,
and holy is her name.
And her surpassing love perdures
from generation to generation
for those who, in meekness, love her.
Her strong arms uplift us,
but those who exalt themselves will be humbled.
She has created a discipleship of equals,
she has filled those who hunger and thirst
after righteousness;
she has exposed the emptiness of material wealth,
she has refreshed those
who are gentle and humble of heart.
She remembers her covenant with us.
She made it with the patriarchs and matriarchs,
Abraham and Sarah and their sons and daughters
for ever and ever. Amen.

J. Massyngbaerde Ford

DISMISSAL AND BLESSING

PRESIDER   Go in peace,
and with your whole heart honor your father;
your mother's birthpangs forget not.
Remember, of these parents you were born;
what can you give them
for all they gave you?

ALL   *Thanks be to God.*

PRESIDER   May God, our Father and our Mother, bless us.

ALL   *Amen.*

CLOSING HYMN

FOR A FATHER

INTRODUCTION   *(For the presider and congregation as they wait for the service to begin.)*

For this service our Scripture readings are taken from the following sources: The psalm is one which praises the parental care of God, one of tenderness and understanding.

The first reading is the story of the prophet Elijah's ascension to heaven. His spiritual son, Elisha, followed him and begged for a portion of his spirit. This was granted, and Elisha was able to perform feats similar to Elijah.

The second reading is taken from the Gospel of John which expresses Jesus' concept of a good father in whom we can trust and who will provide a home for us. Jesus comes to reveal the parenthood of God. This theme is repeated in the third reading, taken from the Gospel of Matthew.

The service closes with "The Benedictus," a modern rendering of the canticle of Zechariah, father of John the Baptist.

OPENING HYMN

PRESIDER   Brothers and sisters, we are gathered for the sacred privilege of saying farewell to a father, a husband, and a friend. Let us listen to the words of Scripture concerning the sanctity of parents.

> Children, pay heed to a father's right;
> do so that you may live.
> For the Lord sets a father in honor over his children;
> a mother's authority he confirms over her sons.

44

He who honors his father atones for sins,
he stores up riches who reveres his mother.

Jesus, himself, frequently spoke about his filial relationship to God. Let us commemorate the parental love of God as expressed in Psalm 103.

Responsorial *(Adapted from Psalm 103:13-18)*

PRESIDER   As tenderly as a father treats his children,
so Yahweh treats those who fear him;
he knows of what we are made,
he remembers that we are dust.

ALL   *As tenderly as a father treats his children.*

PRESIDER   As for a human person—his days are like grass,
he blooms like the wild flowers;
as soon as the wind blows he is gone,
never to be seen there again.

ALL   *As tenderly as a father treats his children.*

PRESIDER   But Yahweh's faithful love for those who fear him
is from eternity and forever;
and his saving justice for their children's children;
as long as they keep his covenant,
and carefully obey his precepts.

ALL   *As tenderly as a father treats his children.*

PRESIDER   Bless, Yahweh, my soul.

Psalm Prayer

PRESIDER   O God, our Father and our Mother,
make us truly grateful and give us glad memories
of our deceased father, N. *(name deceased).*
We thank you for his love,
his support, his understanding,
and his example of Christian fatherhood,
through Jesus Christ, our Lord.

ALL   *Amen.*

PRESIDER   Let us reflect on the Scripture passage that narrates how Elisha prayed for a double portion of his spiritual father's spirit.

FIRST READER   A reading from the second book of Kings (2:1, 8-15).

This is what happened when Yahweh took Elijah up to heaven in the whirlwind...Fifty of the brotherhood of prophets followed them, halting some distance away as the two of them stood beside the Jordan. Elijah took his cloak, rolled it up and struck the water; and the water divided to left and right, and the two of them crossed over dry-shod. When they had crossed, Elijah said to Elisha, "Make your request. What can I do for you before I am snatched away from you?" Elisha answered, "Let me inherit a double portion of your spirit." "Your request is difficult," Elijah said. "If you see me while I am being snatched away from you, it will be as you ask; if not, it will not be so." Now as they walked on, talking as they went, a chariot of fire appeared and horses of fire coming between the two of them; and Elijah went up to heaven in the whirlwind. Elijah saw it, and shouted, "My father! My father! Chariot of Israel and its chargers!" Then he lost sight of him, and taking hold of his own clothes he tore them in half. He picked up Elijah's cloak which had fallen, and went back and stood on the bank of the Jordan.

He took Elijah's cloak and struck the water, "Where is Yahweh, the God of Elijah?" he cried. As he struck the water it divided to right and left, and Elisha crossed over. The brotherhood of prophets saw him in the distance, and said "The spirit of Elijah has come to rest on Elisha; they went to meet him and bowed to the ground before him.

This is the word of the Lord.

ALL   *Thanks be to God.*

SCRIPTURE PRAYER

PRESIDER   O God, father of orphans and defender of widows,
grant us, we beseech you,
a double portion of N.'s spirit
and the discernment and wisdom
to use it rightly,
through Jesus Christ, our Lord.

ALL   *Amen.*

ALTERNATE READING *(Genesis 27:26-29)*

PRESIDER   Isaac said to Jacob, "Come closer, and kiss me, son."
He went closer and kissed his father, who sniffed
the smell of his clothes. Then he blessed him, saying:
"Ah, the smell of my son
is like the smell of a fertile field which Yahweh has
blessed
May God give you
dew from heaven, and the richness of the earth,
abundance of grain and wine!
Let peoples serve you
and nations bow low before you!
Be master of your brothers;
let your mother's other sons bow low before you!
Accursed be whoever curses you
and blessed be whoever blesses you!"

This is the word of the Lord.

ALL   *Thanks be to God.*

PRAYER

FIRST READER   He who honors his father atones for sins;

SECOND READER   He stores up riches who reveres his mother.

FIRST READER   In word and deed honor your father,

SECOND READER   That his blessing may be upon you.

FIRST READER   For a father's blessing gives a family firm roots,

SECOND READER   But a mother's curse uproots the growing plant.

FIRST READER   My son, take care of your father when he is old;

SECOND READER   Grieve him not as long as he lives.

FIRST READER   Even if his mind fail, be considerate with him;

SECOND READER   Revile him not in the fullness of your strength.

FIRST READER   For kindness to a father will not be forgotten,

SECOND READER   Like warmth on frost it will melt away your sins.

PRESIDER   Let us reflect upon the parenthood of God.

SECOND READER   A reading from the Gospel of John (14:1-4; 9-10).

Do not let your hearts be troubled.
You trust in God, trust also in me.
In my Father's house there are many places to live in;
otherwise I would have told you.
I am going now to prepare a place for you,
and after I have gone and prepared you a place,
I shall return to take you to myself,
so that you may be with me
where I am.
You know the way to the place where I am going.

Anyone who has seen me has seen the Father,
    so how can you say, "Show us the Father"?
Do you not believe
that I am in the Father; and the Father is in me?

This is the word of the Lord.

ALL   *Thanks be to God.*

ALTERNATE READING

SECOND READER   A reading from St. Paul's letter to the Ephesians (3:14-21).

This, then, is what I pray, kneeling before the Father, from whom every fatherhood, in heaven or on earth, takes its name. In the abundance of his glory may he, through his Spirit, enable you to grow firm in power with regard to your inner self, so that Christ may live in your hearts through faith, and then, planted in love and built on love, with all God's holy people you will have the strength to grasp the breadth and the length, the height and the depth; so that, knowing the love of Christ, which is beyond knowledge, you may be filled with the utter fullness of God.

Glory be to him whose power, working in us, can do infinitely more than we can ask or imagine; glory be to him from generation to generation in the Church and in Christ Jesus forever and ever. Amen.

This is the word of the Lord.

ALL   *Thanks be to God.*

PRESIDER   God of love,
          hear our prayer for the repose of the soul of N.
          may we remember the privilege of knowing him.

          God of courage,
          let not our energies be drowned in grief.
          Help us to carry on all that was dear
          to N. our father (and husband),

          God of wisdom,
          may we nurture and bring to maturity,
          all that our father showed us
          both by word and example,

          We ask this through Christ, our Lord,

ALL   *Amen.*

PRESIDER   Let us listen to the New Testament reading which speaks of Jesus' filial relationship with God.

THIRD READER   A reading from the Gospel of Matthew (11:25-30).

At that time Jesus exclaimed, "I bless you, Father, Lord of heaven and earth, for hiding these things from the learned and the clever and revealing them to little children. Yes, Father, for that is what it pleased you to do. Everything has been entrusted to me by my Father; and no one knows the Son except the Father just as no one knows the Father except the Son and those to whom the Son chooses to reveal him."

This is the word of the Lord.

ALL   *Thanks be to God.*

PRESIDER   O God, our Father and our Mother,
    your Son came to reveal your parental image to us.
May parents reverence their calling
    and fulfill their parental responsibilities
    with affection and wisdom,
    through Jesus Christ, our Lord and brother,

ALL   *Amen.*

PRAYER OF INTERCESSION AND THANKSGIVING

PRESIDER   Let us present our intercessions to God who is alert to hear the cry of the bereaved:

For the repose of the soul of N., may he rest in peace, and find the fulfillment of that new life which he was given in baptism,

ALL   *God, our Creator, hear us.*

PRESIDER   In thanksgiving for the special gifts of N. *(here some may be specified)*, and for his professional achievements which he combined with his love for his family, may he ever be an inspiration for us,

ALL   *God, our Creator, hear us.*

PRESIDER   For his enjoyment of leisure *(here some activities may be specified)*, may we follow his role model in work and recreation,

ALL   *God, our Creator, hear us.*

PRESIDER   For his wife, N. and their children, N.(s) may the Holy Spirit console them.

ALL   *God, our Creator, hear us.*

PRESIDER   For us, that we may believe that N. continues to live and takes an interest and delight in our lives,

ALL   *God, our Creator, hear us.*

(Here the presider invites spontaneous prayer, and after a suitable pause prays:)

PRESIDER   Jesus, our brother,
      give us faith to believe
      that N. has been welcomed
        into his heavenly home.
    He awaits our joining him
      when we, too, are called.

ALL   *Amen.*

COLLECT *(Prayer for the forgotten)*

PRESIDER   Let us pray for marriage partners who have not been blessed as we have:

FIRST READER   For those fathers who have not accepted the responsibility of paternity,

SECOND READER   May God inspire them to be fathers of orphans.

FIRST READER   For parents injured physically, psychologically or spiritually by their children,

SECOND READER   May they conceive forgiveness, forbearance and generosity.

FIRST READER   For parents bereaved by war and violence,

SECOND READER   May they be granted the peace which passes all understanding.

FIRST READER   For those who have watched their children die of malnutrition, starvation or disease,

SECOND READER   May the world work towards a redistribution of wealth.

PRESIDER   Let us conclude with the song of Zechariah, the father of John the Baptist:

Blessed be the God of Israel,
The ever living Lord,
Who comes in pow'r to save his own,
His people Israel.
For Israel he raises up,
Salvation's tow'r on high
In David's house who reigned as king
And servant of the Lord.

Through holy prophets did he speak
His word in days of old,
That he would save us from our foes
And all who bear us ill.
To our ancestors did he give
His covenant of love
So with us all he keeps his word
In love that knows no end.

Of old he gave his solemn oath
To Father Abraham;
His seed a mighty race should be
And bless'd for ever more.
He vowed to set his people free
From fear of every foe
That we might serve him all our days
In goodness, love and peace.

O tiny child, your name shall be,

The prophet of the Lord:
The way of God you shall prepare
To make his coming known.
You shall proclaim to Israel
Salvation's dawning day
When God shall wipe away all sins
In his redeeming love.

The rising sun shall shine on us
To bring the light of day
To all who sit in darkest night
And shadow of the grave.
Our footsteps God shall safely guide
To walk the ways of peace.
His name for ever more be bless'd
Who lives and loves and saves.

(Translation: James Quinn, SJ)

DISMISSAL AND BLESSING

PRESIDER Go in peace
and with your whole heart honor your father;
your mother's birthpangs forget not.
Remember, of these parents you were born;
what can you give them
for all they gave you?"

ALL *Thanks be to God.*

PRESIDER May God let the light of his face
shine upon you.

ALL *Amen.*

CLOSING HYMN

FOR ONE WHO HAS TAKEN
HIS OR HER OWN LIFE

INTRODUCTION   *(For use of the presider and congregation as they wait for the service to begin.)*

It is not an easy task to prepare a wake service for a person who has taken his or her own life. In the past those who died in this way were not buried in consecrated ground. Today the Church has more understanding, and the new funeral rites provide a prayer for the occasion of such a death. There can be no doubt that the Christian faith cannot condone planned suicide; yet all judgment is in the compassionate and justice-dealing hands of God.

We, too, must seek to have forbearance and compassion for one who, caught up on the bleak billow of despair, could not pilot a frail human nature against such a tempest. Certainly, this is a spiritual shipwreck. But we cannot place the burden on an individual; rather, we place the burden upon society. We pray for society's guilt when we intone "Lamb of God who takes away the sin of the world, have mercy on us." It must be in this spirit of suspension of judgment that we approach this wake service.

The service begins with the recitation of the classical penitential psalm, the psalm which the ancients attributed to David after his sin against Bathsheba and her husband, Uriah. We pray for the forgiveness of sin, witting and unwitting, individual or societal. The response interwoven with this psalm comes from Jesus' words about the woman prostitute found in Luke 7:47.

The first reading is selected from the prophet Hosea, a prophet of compassion and courage who upbraided Israel for her sins, but balanced this by his powerful presentation of divine love. The prayer which follows is taken from the description of the new creation in the Book of Revelation.

The second reading concerns the last rites performed upon the body of Jesus. His body must have been almost unrecognizable after scourging and crucifixion; but Joseph of Arimathea and the women disciples of Jesus were prepared to perform a task which was offensive to every human sense. Perhaps this will help those who were unfortuante enough to find the body of the deceased person for whom we pray today.

Opening Hymn

Welcome

Presider   Brothers and sisters, we meet together in perplexity, confusion and anguish. Some of us may perhaps be burdened with inexplicable guilt. Our brother (sister) N. *(name deceased)* has taken his (her) own life. We gather together to ask for healing and peace. We have great need of the holy spirit of God. Let us first attend to our feelings of guilt, whether these are justified or unjustified. Let us ask for God's forgiveness and that of our community for us and for our deceased brother (sister) in the age old words of King David. He was an impulsive man, capable of great sin but capable also of immense humility, repentance and generosity.

Responsorial *(Adapted from Psalm 51)*

Presider   Have mercy on me, O God, in your faithful love,
in your great tenderness wipe away my offenses;
wash me thoroughly from my guilt,
purify me from my sin.

ALL   *Our sins are forgiven if we have great love.*

PRESIDER   For I am well aware of my offenses,
my sin is constantly in mind.
Against you, you alone, I have sinned.
I have done what you see to be wrong.

ALL   *Our sins are forgiven if we have great love.*

PRESIDER   But you delight in sincerity of heart,
and in secret you teach me wisdom.
Purify me with hyssop till I am clean,
wash me till I am whiter than snow.

ALL   *Our sins are forgiven if we have great love.*

PRESIDER   Let me hear the sound of joy and gladness,
and the bones you have crushed will dance.
Turn away your face from my sins,
and wipe away all my guilt.

ALL   *Our sins are forgiven if we have great love.*

PRESIDER   God, create in me a new heart,
renew within me a resolute spirit,
do not thrust me away from your presence,
do not take away from me your spirit of holiness.
Give me back the joy of your salvation,
sustain in me a generous spirit.

ALL   *Our sins are forgiven if we have great love.*

Psalm Prayer

PRESIDER   God, merciful and compassionate,
you alone know the secrets of the human heart.
Forgive all our sins, witting and unwitting.
Embrace us all
in the warmth of your healing love,
through Jesus Christ, our redeemer,

ALL   *Amen.*

(If a priest is present he may give general absolution).

PRESIDER   God has forgiven all our sins. Let us have the compassion and generosity to forgive ourselves and to
allow ourselves to enter the blessed realm of hope.

FIRST READER   A reading from the book of Hosea (6:1-3).

Come, let us return to Yahweh,
He has rent us and he will heal us;
he has struck us and he will bind up our wounds;
after two days he will revive us,
on the third day he will raise us up
and we shall live in his presence.
Let us know, let us strive to know Yahweh;
that he will come is as certain as the dawn.
He will come to us like a shower,
like the rain of springtime to the earth.

This is the word of the Lord.

ALL   *Thanks be to God.*

Prayer

FIRST READER   Look, here God lives among human beings.

SECOND READER   God will make his home among them.

FIRST READER   They shall be his people,

SECOND READER   And he will be their God.

FIRST READER   He will wipe away all tears from their eyes;

SECOND READER   And there will be no more death.

FIRST READER   And no more mourning or sadness or pain.

SECOND READER   The world of the past has gone.

PRESIDER   Let us pray:

O, God, our Creator,
your Son died
and was raised on the third day.

Give life, joy and peace
to our deceased brother (sister)
  in that place where all anguish of heart
  has fled away,
  through Jesus Christ our Lord,

ALL *Amen.*

PRESIDER Let us hear with hope and joy the Gospel of Luke. As Jesus' bruised and mangled body was laid to rest by good men and women and reverently embalmed with oil and spices, so we lay to rest our brother (sister) who may not always have found peace and rest in this life. He (she) will rise again on the last day with no sorrow.

SECOND READER A reading from the Gospel of Luke (23:50-56; 24:1-6).

And now a member of the Council arrived, a good and upright man named Joseph. He had not consented to what the others had planned and carried out. He came from Arimathea, a Jewish town, and he lived in the hope of seeing the kingdom of God. This man went to Pilate and asked for the body of Jesus. He then took it down, wrapped it in a shroud and put it in a tomb which was hewn in stone and which had never held a body. It was Preparation day and the Sabbath was beginning to grow light.

Meanwhile the women who had come from Galilee with Jesus were following behind. They took note of the tomb and how the body had been laid.

Then they returned and prepared spices and ointments. And on the Sabbath day they rested as the Law required.

On the first day of the week, at the first sign of dawn, they went to the tomb with the spices they had prepared. They found that the stone had been rolled away from the tomb, but on entering they could not find the body of the Lord Jesus. As they stood there puzzled about this, two men in brilliant clothes suddenly appeared at their side. Terrified, the women bowed their heads to the ground. But the two said to them, "Why look among the dead for someone who is alive? He is not here; he has risen."

This is the word of the Lord.

ALL *Thanks be to God.*

PRESIDER Generous God, you raised Jesus from the dead.
Give us rest that we may be healed.
Let a new day dawn for us
  and for our brother (sister).
May our common grief
  unite us in a new community of love.

ALL *Amen.*

PRAYER OF INTERCESSION AND THANKSGIVING

PRESIDER Let us turn to God with our intercessions and prayer. For the family and friends of N. that they may be strengthened and comforted in their tragedy,

ALL *Hear us, gracious God.*

PRESIDER For those who found and looked upon the body of our brother (sister), that gradually their shock and trauma may be healed;

ALL *Hear us, gracious God.*

PRESIDER For us all that God may give us the spirit of understanding, discernment and trust to help to avert similar tragedies,

ALL *Hear us, gracious God.*

PRESIDER For all who may consider taking their own lives, that they may receive the spirit of fortitude to continue to embrace the uncertainties of this life,

ALL *Hear us, gracious God.*

PRESIDER   That we may remember all the joys N. found in life and all that he (she) did to make others happy,

ALL   *Hear us, gracious God.*

PRESIDER   That this catastrophe may not erase from our hearts and minds the joy and challenge which N. found in life (*Or; May we not take this incident as an indication that N.'s life was always sad*), let us pray to the Lord,

ALL   *Hear us, gracious God.*

(Here the congregation is invited to add their prayers for the bereaved, and also in thanksgiving for the special gifts of the deceased. These might be written in advance with the help of the family.)

COLLECT *(Commemoration of the needy)*

PRESIDER   In our grief let us not forget those who have died without the blessings which our friend enjoyed.

FIRST READER   For all those who, in the grip of despair, took their lives,

SECOND READER   May they be filled with the joy and peace which passes all understanding.

FIRST READER   For those who persevere amidst adversities greater than our own,

SECOND READER   May they inspire others with their courage and win peace in the end.

FIRST READER   For those who have died by violence, starvation, or war,

SECOND READER   May they enjoy God's gentleness, his abundance and his peace.

FIRST READER   For all teenagers struggling with the problem of self-identity,

Second Reader   May they rejoice in their unique gifts, unite in their shared gifts and be generous in serving others less privileged than themselves.

First Reader   For those engaged in research to discover the factors contributing to suicidal deaths,

Second Reader   May the spirit of discernment inspire them.

Presider   God of all wisdom,
     we commend into your creative hands
the body and soul
     of our brother (sister) N.
Re-fashion them with love and skill
     and keep within us the lively expectation
     of joyful reunion in heaven,
through Jesus Christ, our Lord and brother,

All   *Amen.*

Dismissal and Blessing

Presider   Go in peace,
     to treasure each moment of life.

All   *Thanks be to God.*

Presider   The courage of the Lord Jesus,
     the compassion of God,
     and discernment of the Holy Spirit
     be with us all.

All   *Amen.*

Closing Hymn

FOR ONE WHO DIES
AFTER A LONG ILLNESS

INTRODUCTION   *(For use of the presider and congregation while waiting for the service to begin.)*

Our service begins with the words of St. Paul written as he waited in prison for his trial and possible death. He sees his life in sacrifical terms, an offering poured out to God for the sake of humankind. He feels he has left no unfinished business and can look forward with confidence to receiving God's blessing on his work. He anticipates this with joy.

The morning "psalm" is taken from Isaiah 38 (*see also 2 Kings 20*). It is said to be the prayer of King Hezekiah when he fell ill.

The first reading is a moving passage from 2 Corinthians. Paul himself was a tent maker, and it is not surprising that he describes our bodies as earthly tents: these will be replaced by a heavenly tent which will never grow old. Paul must also have in mind the presence of God which dwelt in a tent during the travels of the Israelites through the desert for forty years.

In the second reading Jesus compares our present suffering to childbirth. It is, indeed, very painful and frightening. But when the baby is born both parents forget their anxiety and pain; it is swallowed up in their joy as the child comes into the world.

The service ends with the *Nunc Dimittis* (Now Lettest Thou), which is the traditional name of the canticle attributed to Simeon, the elderly priest-prophet who served in the temple of Jerusalem. When he saw the infant Jesus, he was content to die in peace. The canticle suggests that he accepted his death like a sentry who is glad to be relieved of his watching post when he has fulfilled his responsibilities.

Opening Hymn

Welcome

Presider   Friends, St. Paul says in the second letter to Timothy (4:6-8):

> As for me, my life is already being poured away as a libation, and the time has come for me to depart. I have fought the good fight to the end; I have run the race to the finish; I have kept the faith; all there is to come for me now is the crown of uprightness which the Lord, the upright judge, will give me on that Day; and not only to me but to all those who have longed for his appearing.

We are gathered together today to bid farewell to a friend who also fought the good fight and remained faithful. At the beginning of this service let us enter into his (her) sufferings and his (her) joy in healing for a brief moment through the words of Isaiah.

Responsorial *(Adapted from Isaiah 38:9-19)*

Presider   I thought: In the noon of my life
I am to depart.
At the gates of Sheol I shall be held
for the rest of my days.

All   *My bitterness turns to well-being.*

Presider   My home has been pulled up, and thrown away
like a shepherd's tent;
like a weaver, I have rolled up my life,
he has cut me from the loom.

ALL   *My bitterness turns to well-being.*

PRESIDER   From dawn to dark, you have been making an end
of me;
till daybreak, I cried for help;
like a lion, he has crushed all my bones,
from dawn to dark, you have been making an end
of me.

ALL   *My bitterness turns to well-being.*

PRESIDER   The Lord is over them, they live,
and everything in them lives by his spirit.
You will cure me. Restore me to life.
At once my bitterness turns to well-being.

ALL   *My bitterness turns to well-being.*

PRESIDER   For you have preserved my soul
from the pit of nothingness.
The living, the living are the ones who praise you,
as I do today.

ALL   *My bitterness turns to well-being.*

PSALM PRAYER

PRESIDER   O God, our healer, you have called to yourself
our brother (sister) N. (*name deceased*);
as he (she) was born into this world
through the labor of his (her) mother,
so he (she) is initiated into the next world
through his own (her own) suffering and pain.
May his (her) new life
erase every memory of pain,
through Christ, our Lord,

ALL   *Amen.*

PRESIDER   Brothers and sisters, let us hear how, even in our
suffering, God works towards our new creation.

FIRST READER   A reading from the second book of Corinthians (5:1-5).

For we are well aware that when the tent that houses us on earth is folded up, there is a house for us from God, not made by human hands but everlasting, in the heavens. And in this earthly state we do indeed groan, longing to put on our heavenly home over the present one; if indeed we are to be found clothed rather than stripped bare. Yes, indeed, in this present tent, we groan under the burden, not that we want to be stripped of our covering, but because we want to be covered with a second garment on top, so that what is mortal in us may be swallowed up by life. It is God who designed us for this very purpose, and he has given us the Spirit as a pledge.

This is the word of the Lord.

ALL   *Thanks be to God.*

PRAYER

FIRST READER   I know that I have a living defender and he will rise up at last, on the dust of the earth.

SECOND READER   After my awakening, he will set me close to him, and from my flesh I shall look on God.

FIRST READER   He whom I shall see will take my part;

SECOND READER   My eyes will be gazing on no stranger.

PRESIDER   God of understanding,
       even in our bereavement,
       give us courage to rejoice;
    that the sufferings of our friend, N.,
       have led to new life in Jesus Christ

ALL   *Amen.*

PRESIDER   Let us hear with joy the proclamation of the Gospel.

SECOND READER   A reading from the Gospel of John (16:20-22; 28).

In all truth I tell you,
you will be weeping and wailing
while the world will rejoice;
you will be sorrowful
but your sorrow will be turned into joy.
A woman in childbirth suffers,
because her time has come;
but when she gives birth to the child she forgets the suffering
in her joy that a human being has been born into this world.
So it is with you; you are sad now
But I will see you again, and your hearts will be full of joy,
and that joy no one will take from you.
I came from the Father and have come into the world
and now I am leaving the world to go to the Father.

This is the word of the Lord.

ALL   *Thanks be to God.*

PRESIDER   O God, the source of all hope,
grant to all who mourn
a tranquil spirit and sustained hope.
Through Jesus Christ, our Lord,

ALL   *Amen.*

PRAYER OF INTERCESSION AND THANKSGIVING

PRESIDER   Brothers and sisters, we invite you all to give thanks for the privilege of knowing our brother (sister) N.

In thanksgiving for the kindness, compassion and love which N.'s sickness produced in others, especially *(here may be mentioned those who nursed or cared for N.)*,

ALL   *We thank you, our God.*

PRESIDER For the patience, strength and courage which N. showed in his (her) trials and sufferings,

ALL *We thank you, our God.*

PRESIDER For the support of prayer, good wishes and practical help from near and far which supported N. and his (her) family and friends,

ALL *We thank you, our God.*

PRESIDER For the gifts which you bestowed upon N. especially *(here may be mentioned gifts and characteristics of N. which were particularly helpful or appreciated by others),*

ALL *We thank you, our God.*

PRESIDER In thanksgiving for the service of doctors, nurses and ministers who assisted N. in his (her) illness,

ALL *We thank you, our God.*

(A time is offered for personal spontaneous prayer or silent petitions.)

PRESIDER O Lord, our God,
  with consummate art you fashioned the human frame.
You endowed man and woman
  with excellence of mind and soul.
Hear our prayers in thanksgiving
  for our deceased brother (sister).
May his (her) memory never fade,
  may his (her) virtues live on in our own lives.
May he (she) rejoice in his (her) transformed body
  and his (her) peace of mind,

ALL *Amen.*

COLLECT *(Prayer for the forgotten dead)*

PRESIDER In our sorrow let us not forget those less fortunate than ourselves:

FIRST READER   For those who died without the support of friends, and without medical assistance,

SECOND READER   May they have the unending friendship and support of God.

FIRST READER   For those who died homeless, lonely and bewildered, let us pray to the Lord,

SECOND READER   May they know that God has prepared many mansions for them.

FIRST READER   For those who plan to take their own lives, let us pray to the Lord,

SECOND READER   May Christ, who endured the cross, sustain them.

FIRST READER   For those who will die in the midst of conflict and with unfinished affairs,

SECOND READER   May their going forth be in peace.

FIRST READER   For those who will be struck by sudden and unprepared death,

SECOND READER   May the trauma of their family and friends be healed.

PRESIDER   Jesus, our Wounded Healer,
    when the sun set
    you healed the sick who were brought to you.
The sun of N.'s life has set.
Touch him (her),
    bring him (her)
    refreshment of body, peace of mind,
    and joy of soul.

ALL   *Amen.*

PRESIDER   Let us say farewell to our friend in the words of the prophet Simeon:

    Now, Master, you are letting your servant go in
        peace
    for my eyes have seen the salvation

which you have made ready in the sight of the
   nations;
a light of revelation for the gentiles
and the glory of your people Israel.

ALL *Amen.*

DISMISSAL AND BLESSING

PRESIDER Go in peace,
   believing that N. rests in peace and joy.

ALL *Amen.*

PRESIDER The grace of the Wounded Healer be with us all,

ALL *Amen.*

CLOSING HYMN

FOR ONE KILLED
IN A CARELESS ACCIDENT

INTRODUCTION   *(For use of the presider and congregation as they wait for the service to begin.)*

This wake is written for the occasion when death ensues after an accident that appears due to someone's irresponsibility. An example of this would be an accident caused by the driver of a car who was intoxicated or under the influence of drugs.

The mourning psalm is the traditional one used in the office for the dead in the Roman Catholic Church. Whereas we can recognize irresponsibility on this tragic occasion, in the psalm we admit that the whole human race can err, and we plead with God to help us all.

In the first reading we see how the apostle, Paul, called on the Roman Christians for courage and humanity of the highest order. He shows us the true Christian conduct in the face of people who harm us. But we cannot expect to acquire this disposition immediately. We must be patient with ourselves and try to grow little by little.

The responsorial is also taken from the words of Paul, written from the depth of his heart when he considered the great tragedies that befell him in his missionary work. In spite of these he managed, with the grace of God, to endure and to continue to hope.

The Gospel passage tells how the early Christians found it hard to believe that Christ, their teacher, who had died a violent and cruel death, could be risen from the dead. We must try to believe that our deceased friend will also rise again, and every wound and scar be healed.

The farewell is a short hymn which appears to have been quoted either by Paul or one of his disciples, in a letter to Timothy in Ephesus.

OPENING **H**YMN

WELCOME

PRESIDER   Brothers and sisters, we are met to mourn the untimely death of our beloved N. This death is more tragic than many deaths, because it is unnecessary and unnatural, the result of human folly. We have greater need of understanding and of compassion than many of those who are bereaved. It is not strange if we feel anger and disgust as well as sorrow. Let us pour out our complaint before God, whose Son also met an untimely, unnecessary and violent death, the result, too, of human frailty and sin.

RESPONSORIAL *(Adapted from Psalm 130)*

PRESIDER   From the depths I call to you, Yahweh,
            Lord, hear my cry.
            Listen attentively
            to the sound of my pleading!

ALL   *Comfort me over and over.*

PRESIDER   If you kept a record of our sins,
            Lord, who could stand their ground?
            But with you is forgiveness,
            that you may be revered.

ALL   *Comfort me over and over.*

PRESIDER   I rely, my whole being relies,
            Yahweh, on your promise.
            My whole being hopes in the Lord,
            more than watchmen for daybreak
            let Israel hope in Yahweh.

ALL   *Comfort me over and over.*

PRESIDER   For with Yahweh is faithful love,
            with him generous ransom;

and he will ransom Israel
from all its sins.

ALL   *Comfort me over and over.*

PSALM PRAYER

PRESIDER   God of consolation and understanding,
help us to free our pent-up emotions before you.
Enfold us in your patience
and speak tenderly to our hearts,
through Jesus Christ, our Lord.

ALL   *Amen.*

PRESIDER   Let us reflect upon the words of Paul to the Jews and Christians in Rome who were often subject to cruelty, ridicule and injustice from higher authorities.

FIRST READER   A reading from Paul's letter to the Romans (12:15-21).

Bless your persecutors; never curse them, bless them. Rejoice with others when they rejoice, and be sad with those in sorrow. Give the same consideration to all others alike. Pay no regard to social standing, but meet humble people on their own terms. Do not congratulate yourself on your own wisdom. Never pay back evil with evil, but bear in mind the ideas that all regard with respect. As much as is possible, and to the utmost of your ability, be at peace with everyone. Never try to get revenge: leave that, my dear friends, to the Retribution. As Scripture says: Vengeance is mine—I will pay them back, the Lord promises. And more: if your enemy is hungry, give him (her) something to eat; if thirsty, something to drink. By this, you will be heaping red-hot coals on his (her) head. Do not be mastered by evil, but master evil with good.

This is the word of the Lord.

ALL   *Thanks be to God.*

PRESIDER   Brothers and sisters, we have received a challenge
to forgive in the face of horrendous irresponsibility.
We can accept it only by the grace of our Lord Jesus
Christ who said, as he was fastened to the cross of
shame, "Father, forgive them, they know not what
they do."
Let us pray:

Creator of all,
   you have promised not to give us temptation
   beyond our strength.
If we cannot accept your challenge now,
   give us grace to grow in heroic love,
   step by step, day by day,
   until we can say,
"Father, forgive him (her),
   he (she) knew not what he (she) did"
   through Jesus Christ, our Lord and brother,

ALL   *Amen.*

PRAYER *(Adapted from 2 Corinthians 4:7-15)*

FIRST READER   We are subjected to every kind of hardship,

SECOND READER   But never distressed;

FIRST READER   We see no way out,

SECOND READER   But we never despair;

FIRST READER   We are pursued,

SECOND READER   But never cut off;

FIRST READER   Knocked down,

SECOND READER   But still have some life in us;

FIRST READER   Always we carry with us in our body the death of
Jesus,

SECOND READER   So that the life of Jesus, too, may be visible in our body.

FIRST READER   But we have the same spirit of faith as is described in scripture—*I believed and therefore I spoke*—

SECOND READER   We, too, speak, realizing that he who raised up the Lord Jesus will raise us up with Jesus in our turn.

FIRST READER   And bring us to himself—and you as well.

PRESIDER   God of strength,
        comfort us in our distress
        and fill us with the realization
    that our beloved N.
        dwells with you in happiness and peace;
    and has extended forgiveness
        to the one who caused his (her) death,
        through Jesus Christ, our Lord,

ALL   *Amen.*

SECOND READER   A reading from the Gospel of Luke (24:36-43).

The disciples were still talking about all this when Jesus himself stood among them and said to them, "Peace be with you!" In a state of alarm and fright, they thought they were seeing a ghost. But he said, "Why are you so agitated, and why are these doubts stirring in your hearts? See by my hands and my feet that it is I myself. Touch me and see for yourselves; a ghost has no flesh and bones as you can see I have." And as he said this he showed them his hands and his feet. Their joy was so great that they still could not believe it, as they were dumbfounded; so he said to them, "Have you anything here to eat?" And they offered him a piece of grilled fish, which he took and ate before their eyes.

This is the word of the Lord.

ALL   *Thanks be to God.*

PRESIDER God of the risen Jesus,
    help us to realize that N.'s life
    is changed, not taken away.
    When our time comes
        may we be reunited to him (her)
        through Jesus Christ, our Lord,

ALL *Amen.*

PRAYER OF INTERCESSION AND THANKSGIVING

PRESIDER Brothers and sisters, we invite you all to pray for the repose of N's soul; For repentance and grace for the one who caused his (her) death, and for the consolation of the bereaved.

ALL *Merciful God, hear our prayer.*

PRESIDER That our beloved N. may rest in peace and share with us the forgiveness of his (her) killer;

ALL *Merciful God, hear our prayer.*

PRESIDER For the person who caused this tragedy, that he (she) may realize the consequence of his (her) deed and, by the grace of God, live a fruitful life and lead many to reform.

ALL *Merciful God, hear our prayer.*

PRESIDER For alcoholics and drug addicts, that they may be given the insight and strength to live a grace-filled life.

ALL *Merciful God, hear our prayer.*

PRESIDER For members of the Alcoholics Anonymous and similar groups, that God may bless their work and make it fruitful,

ALL *Merciful God, hear our prayer.*

PRESIDER For ourselves that we may always seek to live responsible lives, reverencing creation in all its forms,

ALL   *Merciful God, hear our prayer.*

PRESIDER   For the family and friends of N ., that they may be supported by human and divine consolation,

ALL   *Merciful God, hear our prayer.*

(The congregation is invited to express their petitions and thanksgiving in their own words.)

PRESIDER   O God to whom all hearts are open,
your spirit helps our infirmity
for we know not how to pray.
Speak to our secret thoughts and inward being
and grant us healing and encouragement,
through Christ, our Lord,

ALL   *Amen.*

COLLECT *(Prayer for the forgotten)*

PRESIDER   In our overwhelming grief let us not be forgetful of others who are bereaved and wounded.

FIRST READER   For the dead through war, famine, or plague,

SECOND READER   May they be brought to a land of peace, plenty, and healing.

FIRST READER   For the dead through negligence,

SECOND READER   May the tenderness of God enfold them.

FIRST READER   For the missing dead,

SECOND READER   May their families have human and divine support.

FIRST READER   For the parents of the stillborn,

SECOND READER   May the spirit breathe comfort into them.

PRESIDER   Let us say farewell to our friend in the words St. Paul wrote to Timothy:

If we have died with him, then we shall live with him.

If we persevere, then we shall reign with him.
If we disown him, then he will disown us.
If we are faithless, he is faithful still,
    for he cannot disown his own self.

DISMISSAL AND BLESSING

PRESIDER   Go in peace and be
            open to human and divine compassion.

ALL   *Amen.*

PRESIDER   May the God of all grace
            who called you to eternal glory in Christ
            restore you, confirm you,
            strengthen and support you.
            His power lasts for ever and ever.

ALL   *Amen.*

CLOSING HYMN

FOR A RELIGIOUS LEADER OR TEACHER

INTRODUCTION   *(For the use of the presider and congregation before the service begins.)*

A religious leader or a teacher is one who facilitates the gifts and the fruits of the Spirit in others, as it were, cultivating and nourishing them. Our responsorial psalm reflects the care a leader shows to his or her protegés.

The first reading portrays a person who lives an intimate life with God and shares this with various persons and communities. The response to this reading recalls the beatitudes pronounced by Jesus in the Sermon on the Mount. These clearly display the characteristics of true members of his kingdom.

The second reading describes a few of the gifts of the Spirit which can be attributed to many persons blessed by God.

The Gospel reading recounts the occasion when the risen Christ blessed his men and women disciples and sent them forth to evangelize all nations. Christ then ascended into heaven.

OPENING HYMN

WELCOME

PRESIDER   Brothers and sisters, before Jesus returned to God he said farewell to his friends and disciples. He gave them his blessing and promised them the gift of the Holy Spirit. He bade them spread the good news of the Gospel and not cling to him. We have met to say farewell to a leader of our community and to ask for the strength to continue his (her) work. Let us begin by reciting Psalm 23, which talks about the good shepherd. In the ancient world shepherd was a synonym for leader.

Responsorial *(Adapted from Psalm 23)*

PRESIDER Yahweh is my shepherd, I lack nothing.
In grassy meadows he lets me lie.

ALL *Kindness and faithful love pursue me.*

PRESIDER By tranquil streams he leads me
to restore my spirit.
He guides me in paths of saving justice
as befits his name.

ALL *Kindness and faithful love pursue me.*

PRESIDER Even were I to walk in a ravine as dark as death
I should fear no danger, for you are at my side.
Your staff and your crook are there to soothe me.

ALL *Kindness and faithful love pursue me.*

PRESIDER You prepare a table for me
under the eyes of my enemies;
you anoint my head with oil;
my cup brims over.

ALL *Kindness and faithful love pursue me.*

PRESIDER Kindness and faithful love pursue me
every day of my life.
I make my home in the house of Yahweh
for all time to come.

ALL *Kindness and faithful love pursue me.*

Psalm Prayer

PRESIDER O God, our Good Shepherd,
we thank you for the leadership
and example of our friend N. *(name deceased)*.
May he (she) receive the faithful servant's reward.
May your home now be his (hers)
for all time to come,
through Jesus Christ, our Good Shepherd,

ALL   *Amen.*

PRESIDER   Let us reflect on wise leadership as it is presented in the Wisdom literature.

FIRST READER   A reading from the book of Ecclesiasticus (39:1-15). *(The feminine pronoun may be substituted for the masculine.)*

He researches into the wisdom of all the Ancients,
    he occupies his time with the prophecies.
He preserves the discourses of famous persons,
    he is at home with the niceties of parables.
He researches into the hidden sense of proverbs,
    he ponders the obscurities of parables.
He enters in the service of princes,
    he is seen in the presence of rulers.
He travels in foreign countries,
    he has experienced human good and human evil.
At dawn and with all his heart
    he turns to the Lord his Creator;
He pleads in the presence of the Most High,
    he opens his mouth in prayer
    and makes entreaty for his sins.
If such be the will of the Lord,
    he will be filled with the spirit of intelligence,
He will shower forth words of wisdom,
    and in prayer give thanks to the Lord.
He will grow upright in purpose and learning,
    he will ponder the Lord's hidden mysteries.
He will display the instruction he has received
    taking his pride in the Law of the Lord's covenant.
Many will praise his intelligence
    and it will never be forgotten.
His memory will not disappear,
    generation after generation his name will live.
Nations will proclaim his wisdom,
    the assembly will celebrate his praises.

If he lives long, his name will be more glorious
    than a thousand others,
and if he dies, that will satisfy him just as well.

This is the word of the Lord.

All   *Thanks be to God.*

Alternate Reading *(For a more practical person)*

First Reader   A reading from Sirach 38:31-34

All these people rely on their hands
    and each is skilled at his own craft.
A town could not be inhabited without them,
    there would be no settling, no traveling.
But you will not find them in the parliament,
    they do not hold high rank in the assembly.
They do not sit on the judicial bench,
    and they do not meditate on the Law.
They are not remarkable for their culture or
    judgment,
    nor are they found frequenting the philosophers.
They sustain the structure of the world,
    and their prayer is concerned with their trade.

This is the word of the Lord.

All   *Thanks be to God.*

Presider   O, God of wisdom,
    we thank you for the gifts
    which you gave our friend N.
May we treasure them.
May they bear fruit in our lives,
    through Jesus Christ, our Lord,

All   *Amen.*

PRAYER

FIRST READER   How blessed are the poor in spirit,
the kingdom of heaven is theirs.

SECOND READER   Blessed are the gentle,
they will have the earth as inheritance.

FIRST READER   Blessed are those who mourn;
they shall be comforted.

SECOND READER   Blessed are those who hunger and thirst for
righteousness; they shall have their fill.

FIRST READER   Blessed are the merciful;
they shall have mercy shown them.

SECOND READER   Blessed are the pure in heart;
they shall see God.

FIRST READER   Blessed are the peacemakers;
they shall be recognized as children of God.

SECOND READER   Blessed are those who are presecuted for the cause
of righteousness; the kingdom of heaven is theirs.

SECOND READER   A reading from St. Paul's first epistle to the Corinthians (12:4-11).

There are many different gifts, but it is always the
same Spirit; there are many different ways of serving, but it is always the same Lord. There are many
different forms of activity, but in everybody it is the
same God who is at work in them all. The particular
manifestation of the Spirit granted to each one is to
be used for the general good. To one is given from
the Spirit the gift of utterance expressing wisdom;
to another the gift of utterance expressing
knowledge, in accordance with the same Spirit; to
another, faith, from the same Spirit; and to another,
the gifts of healing, through this one Spirit; to
another, the working of miracles; to another, pro-
phecy; to another, the power of distinguishing

spirits; to one, the gift of different tongues and to another, the interpretation of tongues. But at work in all these is one and the same Spirit, distributing them at will to each individual.

This is the word of the Lord.

All   *Thanks be to God.*

PRAYER

PRESIDER   O God, prodigal in your love,
       we thank you for the many manifestations
          of your Spirit
       in the human community.
    Teach us to cultivate these gifts
       in the spirit of humble and selfless joy,
          through Jesus Christ, our Lord,

All   *Amen.*

PRESIDER   Let us hear the words of Matthew, that tell us how Jesus blessed and commissioned his disciples before he returned to God.

THIRD READER   A reading from the Gospel of Matthew (28:16-20).

Meanwhile the eleven disciples set out for Galilee, to the mountain where Jesus had arranged to meet them. When they saw him they fell down before him, though some hesitated. Jesus came up and spoke to them. He said, "All authority in heaven and on earth has been given to me. Go, therefore, make disciples of all nations; baptize them in the name of the Father and of the Son and of the Holy Spirit, and teach them to observe all the commands I gave you. And look, I am with you always; yes, to the end of time."

This is the word of the Lord.

All   *Thanks be to God.*

PRESIDER   God of all consolation,
            comfort and strengthen those
            whom N. has left on this earth.
            May their joy be in recalling
            the good things bequeathed by N.
            and may the Lord Jesus be with us all,
            even to the end of time.

ALL   *Amen.*

PRAYER OF INTERCESSION AND THANKSGIVING

PRESIDER   Brothers and sisters, we invite you all to pray for the repose of N.'s soul and to give thanks for the privilege of knowing him (her).

            That God will give N. the reward of his (her) labors,

ALL   *Lord, hear our prayer.*

PRESIDER   That our community may remain united even in the physical absence of N.,

ALL   *Lord, hear our prayer.*

PRESIDER   That God may raise up for us, for our church and our nation, leaders like N.,

ALL   *Lord, hear our prayer.*

PRESIDER   That each one of us may recognize the gifts of the Holy Spirit within us and have the courage to use them,

ALL   *Lord, hear our prayer.*

PRESIDER   That we may be deeply convinced that through the resurrection of Jesus we and N. will attain everlasting life.

ALL   *Lord, hear our prayer.*

            (The congregation is invited to express their petitions and thanksgiving in their own words.)

PRESIDER   O Lord our God, our intimate friend,
you have called each man and woman
to a special vocation and destiny.
Grant us discernment to know your will
and the courage to embrace our uniqueness.

ALL   *Amen.*

COLLECT *(Prayer for the forgotten)*

PRESIDER   In our grief let us not be forgetful of others who may
enjoy fewer privileges than we.

FIRST READER   For those who have died alone, unnoticed,
unmourned,

SECOND READER   May they enjoy the communion of saints.

FIRST READER   For those communities which are leaderless and
blown about by every wind of change,

SECOND READER   May the Holy Spirit guide them.

FIRST READER   For those who are imprisoned or persecuted for the
ideals which they plan or implement,

SECOND READER   May God bless their fortitude.

FIRST READER   For the unlettered and the underprivileged, that they
may be empowered,

SECOND READER   May they be taught by the Spirit.

PRESIDER   Let us say farewell to our friend in the words of the
priest and prophet Simeon:

Now, Master, you are letting your servant go in
peace
as you promised;
for my eyes have seen the salvation
which you have made ready in the sight of the
nations;
a light of revelation for gentiles
and the glory of your people Israel.

ALTERNATE PRAYER *(The Song of Mary)*

And, I, in the dignity of Christian womanhood, say:
My soul does magnify our God
and my spirit rejoices in God my savior,
for, in my human fraility, the Spirit, our Mother,
has chosen me.
For, behold, from now on all generations will bless
her gift within me.
For she who is all powerful has empowered me,
and holy is her name.
And her surpassing love perdures
from generation to generation
for those who in meekness love her.
Her strong arms uplift us,
but those who exalt themselves will be humbled.
She has created a discipleship of equals,
she has filled those who hunger and thirst
after righteousness;
she has exposed the emptiness of material wealth,
she has refreshed those
who are gentle and humble of heart.
She remembers her covenant with us.
She made it with the patriarchs and matriarchs,
Abraham and Sarah and their sons and daughters
for ever and ever.

(J. Massyngbaerde Ford).

ALL   *Amen.*

DISMISSAL AND BLESSING

PRESIDER   Go in peace,
            to follow in the footsteps of N.

ALL   *Amen.*

PRESIDER   The grace of our Lord Jesus Christ,
                and the love of God,
                and the fellowship of the Holy Spirit
                be with you all.

ALL   *Amen.*

CLOSING HYMN

For One Who Has Died
in a Violent Manner

Introduction *(For the use of the presider and the congregation while waiting for the service to begin)*

The person who dies a violent death shares in a unique way in the passion, death, and resurrection of Jesus. In order to unite himself with the most abused people in human society, Jesus chose to die one of the most shameful and painful forms of death in his contemporary society. He was crucified like a common slave-criminal; a slave was normally deprived of every human dignity. It is, therefore, Jesus to whom we should turn both for consolation and understanding in our present loss.

The responsorial psalm is a reflection on Jesus' nonviolent response to cruelty. The second reading is taken from 2 Corinthians 4:7-15. In this passage St. Paul reflects upon his personal suffering for the cause of Christ and his gospel. The Gospel foreshadows the violent death of Peter, also thought to be through crucifixion.

We pray that our friend, a victim of violence, may have communion with Jesus and with all martyrs for their faith, both past and present.

Opening Hymn

Welcome

Presider Brothers and sisters, death is always tragic. Today, however, we are faced with more than tragedy. Our beloved N. *(name deceased)* had been killed, it would seem, through wanton cruelty. Our grief is no ordinary grief. We stand in need of maximum help and comfort from other people and from God. God's only beloved Son died one of the most violent deaths in human history. In this situation let us pour out our complaints before God, whose heart understands the most uncontrolled grief and emotion.

RESPONSORIAL *(Adapted from Psalm 31)*

PRESIDER   In you Yahweh, I have taken refuge,
    let me never be put to shame,
in your saving justice deliver me, rescue me,
    turn your ear to me, make haste.

ALL   *Comfort me over and over.*

PRESIDER   Draw me out of the net they have spread for me,
    for you are my refuge;
to your hand I commit my spirit,
    by you have I been redeemed.

ALL   *Comfort me over and over.*

PRESIDER   Take pity on me, Yahweh,
    for I am in trouble.
Vexation is gnawing away my eyes,
    my soul deep within me.

ALL   *Comfort me over and over.*

PRESIDER   For my life is worn out with sorrow,
    and my years with sighs,
My strength gives away under my misery,
    and my bones are all wasted away.

ALL   *Comfort me over and over.*

PRESIDER   But my trust is in you, Yahweh;
    I say, "You are my God,"

every moment of my life is in your hands, rescue me
  from the clutches of my foes who pursue me;
let your face shine on your servant,
  save me in your faithful love.

ALL   *Comfort me over and over.*

PRESIDER   Yahweh, what quantities of good things,
  you have in store for those who fear you,
and bestow on those who make you their refuge,
  for all humanity to see.

ALL   *Comfort me over and over.*

PSALM PRAYER

PRESIDER   God of Job and of all those who suffer
  look with your eye of compassion
  upon this bereaved family and these friends.
Hear them as you heard Job, loud in his complaint,
  and bring them safely
  through the valley of the shadow of death.

ALL   *Amen.*

PRESIDER   Our circumstances in our bereavement are not unlike
those of the relatives of martyrs for the faith. Let us
reflect upon a Jewish mother who witnessed her
seven sons cruelly killed in one day. She was sustained by her hope in the resurrection of the dead.

FIRST READER   A reading from the second book of Maccabees
(7:20-23).

But the mother was especially admirable and worthy of honorable remembrance, for she watched the
death of seven sons in the course of a single day,
and bravely endured it because of her hopes in the
Lord. Indeed she encouraged each of them in their
ancestral tongue; filled with noble conviction, she
reinforced her argument with courage, saying to

them: "I do not know how you appeared in my womb; it was not I who endowed you with breath and life, I had not the shaping of your every part. And hence, the Creator of the world, who made everyone and ordained the origin of all things, will in his mercy give you back breath and life, since for the sake of his laws you have no concern for yourselves."

This is the word of the Lord.

ALL *Thanks be to God.*

ALTERNATE READING *(For an elderly person. 2 Maccabees 6:18, 23-28; 30-31).*

Eleazar, one of the foremost teachers of the Law, a man already advanced in years and of most noble appearance...having taken a noble decision worthy of his years and the dignity of his great age and the well-earned distinction of his grey hairs, worthy too of his impeccable conduct from boyhood, and above all of the holy legislation established by God himself, he answered accordingly: "Pretense," he said, "does not befit our time of life; many young people would suppose that Eleazar at the age of ninety had conformed to the foreigners' way of life and, because I had played this part for the sake of a paltry brief spell of life, might themselves be led astray on my account; I should only bring defilement and disgrace on my old age. Even though for the moment I avoid execution by man, I can never, living or dead, elude the grasp of the Almighty. Therefore if I am man enough to quit this life here and now, I shall prove myself worthy of my old age, and I shall have left the young a noble example of how to make a good death, eagerly and generously for the venerable and holy laws... the Lord whose knowledge is holy sees clearly that, though I might have escaped death, from awe of him I gladly endure these agonies of body in my soul I am glad to suffer."

This was how he died, leaving his death as an example of nobility and a record of virtue not only for the young but for the greater part of the nation.

This is the word of the Lord.

ALL   *Thanks be to God.*

PRAYER *(Adapted from 1 Peter 2:21-25)*

FIRST READER   Follow in Christ's steps.

SECOND READER   He had done nothing wrong, and had spoken no deceit.

FIRST READER   He was insulted and did not retaliate with insults;

SECOND READER   When he was suffering he made no threats, but put his trust in the upright judge.

FIRST READER   He was bearing our sins in his own body on the cross,

SECOND READER   So that we might die to our sins and live for uprightness; through his bruises we have been healed.

FIRST READER   You had gone astray like sheep,

SECOND READER   But now you have returned to the shepherd and guardian of your souls.

SECOND READER   A reading from St. Paul's second letter to the Corinthians (4:7-15).

But we hold this treasure in pots of earthenware, so that the immensity of the power is God's and not our own. We are subjected to every kind of hardship, but never distressed; we see no way out but we never despair; we are pursued but never cut off; knocked down, but still have some life in us; always we carry with us in our body the death of Jesus so that the life of Jesus, too, may be visible in our body. Indeed, while we are still alive, we are continually being handed over to death, for the sake of Jesus, so that the life of Jesus, too, may be visible in our mortal flesh. In us, then, death is at work; in you, life.

But as we have the same spirit of faith as is described in scripture - *I believed and therefore I spoke* - we, too, believe and therefore, we, too, speak, realizing that he who raised up the Lord Jesus will raise us up with Jesus in our turn, and bring us to himself—and you as well. You see, everything is for your benefit, so that as grace spreads, so, to the glory of God, thanksgiving may also overflow among more and more people.

This is the word of the Lord.

ALL   *Thanks be to God.*

PRESIDER   Let us pray in the words of Hannah, the mother of the prophet, Samuel:

O God, our strength and comfort,
    there is no god like you.
You cast down to the nether world
    and raise up again;
    you raise the needy from the dust.
Bless the sleep of the just and
    guard the footsteps of the faithful.
Refresh us with your presence.

ALL   *Amen.*

THIRD READER   A reading from the Gospel of John (21:9-19).

As soon as they had come ashore they saw that there was some bread there and a charcoal fire with fish cooking on it. Jesus said "Bring some of the fish you have just caught." Simon Peter went abroad and dragged the net ashore, full of big fish, one hundred and fifty-three of them; and in spite of there being so many the net was not broken. Jesus said to them, "Come and have breakfast." None of the disciples was bold enough to ask, "Who are you?"; they knew quite well it was the Lord. Jesus then stepped forward, took the bread and gave it to them, and the same with the fish. This was the third time that Jesus revealed himself to the disciples after rising from the dead.

When they had eaten, Jesus said to Simon Peter, "Simon son of John, do you love me more than these others do?" He answered, "Yes, Lord, you know I love you." Jesus said to him, "Feed my lambs." A second time he said to him "Simon son of John, do you love me?" He replied, "Yes, Lord, you know I love you." Jesus said to him, "Look after my sheep." Then he said to him a third time, "Simon son of John, do you love me?" Peter was hurt that he asked him a third time "Do you love me?" and said, "Lord, you know everything; you know I love you." Jesus said to him, "Feed my sheep.

In all truth I tell you,
when you were young
you put on your own belt
and walked where you liked;
but when you grow old
you will stretch out your hands,
and somebody else will put a belt round you
and take you where you would rather not go."

In these words he indicated the kind of death by which Peter would give glory to God. After this he said, "Follow me."

This is the word of the Lord.

ALL   *Thanks be to God.*

PRESIDER   O God, our Father and our Mother,

your beloved Son died a violent death
to conquer death.
Grant that your friend
who shared the manner of your death,
may share also the manner of your resurrection,
through Jesus Christ, our Lord.

ALL   *Amen.*

PRAYER OF INTERCESSION AND THANKSGIVING

PRESIDER   In all our distress let us not forget the good things
we enjoyed with N.

In thanksgiving for the life of N., especially for *(here
mention some personal quality of the deceased)*, may we
hallow his (her) memory by following his (her) good
example,

ALL   *Lord, hear our prayer.*

PRESIDER   For the one who caused the violent death of N, that
the Spirit of gentleness and contrition may enter him
(her),

ALL   *Lord, hear our prayer.*

PRESIDER   For the removal of violence, war, brutality and in-
humane conduct from the world, and from the com-
munication media,

ALL   *Lord, hear our prayer.*

PRESIDER   For the repose of the souls of all who died through
violence,

ALL   *Lord, hear our prayer.*

*(The congregation is invited to express their petitions and
thanksgiving in their own words.)*

PRESIDER   God of all justice,
in your hands are life and death,
resurrection and hope.

Grant that we be not dwarfed
by this tragedy,
but increase in faith, in hope, and in love.
May the loss of N.'s life inspire us
to work with perseverance
for a world of harmony, happiness, and peace,
through Jesus Christ, our Lord.

ALL   *Amen.*

COLLECT *(Prayer for the forgotten)*

PRESIDER   In our great grief let us not be forgetful of others who have endured suffering and violence.

FIRST READER   For all the unborn, who have died violently;

SECOND READER   May they enjoy the full life of heaven.

FIRST READER   For those who have known no life which lacks violence,

SECOND READER   May the Wounded Healer embrace them.

FIRST READER   For those whose souls are seared by verbal violence,

SECOND READER   May they know that a gracious mouth multiples friends.

FIRST READER   For those who have known no violence,

SECOND READER   May God give them an understanding heart.

PRESIDER   Let us say farewell to our friend in words from the book of Wisdom (4:7-8):

The upright, though he die before his time, will find rest. Length of days is not what makes age honorable, nor number of years the true measure of life; understanding, this is grey hairs, untarnished life, this is ripe old age.

Dismissal and Blessing

PRESIDER Go in peace,
          to be harbingers of peace.

ALL *Amen.*

PRESIDER May the Lord bless you and keep you!
          The Lord let his face shine upon you
              and be gracious to you.
          The Lord look upon you kindly
              and give you peace!

ALL *Amen.*

Closing Hymn

ABOUT THE AUTHOR

Dr. J. Massyngbaerde Ford teaches New Testament Studies at the University of Notre Dame, Indiana. Formerly, she held positions in England and Africa. She is also a trained nurse and has had the privilege of performing the Last Offices for the deceased. Her American family comprises four horses, a malemute, and a cat. Her latest book is *Bonded with the Immortal: A Pastoral Introduction to the New Testament* (Michael Glazier, 1987).